The Last Colony in Africa

The Last Colony in Africa

Diplomacy and the Independence of Rhodesia

MICHAEL CHARLTON

Basil Blackwell

First published 1990

Basil Blackwell Ltd
108 Cowley Road, Oxford, OX4 1JF, UK

Basil Blackwell, Inc.
3 Cambridge Center
Cambridge, Massachusetts 02142, USA

British Library Cataloguing in Publication Data

A CIP catalogue record for this book is available from the British Library.

Library of Congress Cataloging in Publication Data

Charlton, Michael.
The last colony in Africa: diplomacy and the independence of Rhodesia/Michael Charlton.
p. cm.
Includes bibliographical references.
ISBN 0–631–17044–8
1. Zimbabwe – History – Chimurenga War, 1966–1980 – Peace.
2. Zimbabwe – History – Chimurenga War, 1966–1980 – Diplomatic history. 3. Zimbabwe – Foreign relations – Great Britain.
4. Great Britain – Foreign relations – Zimbabwe. I. Title.
DT2994.C48 1990
327.689041'09'045 – dc20 89–28286
CIP

Typeset in 10½ on 12pt Ehrhardt
by Wessex Typesetters
(Division of The Eastern Press Ltd)
Frome, Somerset
Printed in Great Britain by
Billing & Sons Ltd, Worcester

Contents

Preface

This book is an oral history of a few months of remarkable diplomacy which ended a protracted conflict of many years' duration and brought an internationally recognized independence to Rhodesia, the last colony in Africa.

The success of this diplomacy has cast long shadows over other apparently intractable disputes, from Africa's deepest south to the Middle East, and the ancestral and prophesying voice of the diplomatist has felt entitled to say 'You never know.'

The contributors to this oral history are the British ministers who had charge of the policy; senior officials of the Foreign and Commonwealth Office; Presidents of the African states; leaders, black and white, of Rhodesia itself; and the leader for South Africa. These are the men to whom it fell to make the crucial decisions which led to the final settlement. This recounting by them of how, and why, they acted as they did marks, in effect, the last part of a great historical movement – the passing of the British empire.

Kipling, who saw the English and their marvellous achievement over the past four centuries 'from the outside', as it were, had long ago felt in his bones what was coming. 'Far called our navies melt away, on dune and headland sink the fire,' he hymned in 'Recessional'. Kipling was Cecil Rhodes's friend: they had met at the Cape, in 1891, when Rhodes had just founded his new colony of Rhodesia. Rhodes, who 'had a habit of jerking out sudden questions', had asked: 'What's your dream?' 'I answered', said Kipling, 'that he was part of it.'[1] We have Kipling's word for it that Cecil Rhodes was largely inarticulate: 'My use to him was mainly as a purveyor of words.' And, as Kipling wrote in his memorial poem on Rhodes's death and his burial in the Matopos hills near

1 In Kipling's autobiographical work, *Something of Myself* (London, Macmillan, 1965).

Bulawayo in 1902, 'The travail of his spirit bred cities in place of speech.'[2]

It was the loss of this spirit which was at the heart of the real sense of loss felt by the British. It was what made Rhodesia a subjective and emotional issue for so long in British politics, even more than beating retreat before the forces of Africanization from the broad streets and sunlit life which Rhodes's visionary eye had carved out of Africa. Kipling's premonitions had, of course, suggested that the British nation needed reorganizing more than the empire had done. The settlement of the Rhodesian question, achieved in 1980, belongs to a time when the British had brought themselves as a nation to undertake that task. Bringing to an end the inveterate bitterness aroused by the issue of Rhodesia formed part of it.

By 1979, Rhodesia posed for the British, in its most acute form, the problem of responsibility without real power. The odds at the outset had seemed overwhelmingly against obtaining a comprehensive agreement. What follows is the story of why an issue which seemed to have assumed its own subjection to fate yielded to this one last effort. Those who brought about or helped to shape the final result, tell it in their own words. No alterations have been made, other than in those occasional instances where the conventions of the spoken word have been thought to require clarification. The contributors were provided with the areas only of questions in advance, and, with that, the opportunity to consult personal diaries and papers. The interviews were recorded between November 1987 and January of the following year, and were originally broadcast in 1988 as a series of six programmes by BBC Radio Three. It has been possible to include additional exchanges from the interviews which were necessarily omitted from the broadcasts because of the constraints of time in broadcasting.

Gratitude is due on several counts. My own and the BBC's go first to the distinguished contributors themselves who gave their time and their recollections. It is also due, in particular to George Fischer, then the Head of Talks and Documentary Programmes at Broadcasting House, who believed it important to document the workings of statecraft which underpin day to day events; and, finally, to Michael Stevenson, who produced the original broadcasts for Radio Three and who was, throughout, a most agreeable and stimulating colleague.

Michael Charlton
Broadcasting House, London

2 Rudyard Kipling, 'The Burial'.

The Contributors

RT HON. JULIAN AMERY MP Secretary of State for Air, 1960–2; Minister of State, Foreign and Commonwealth Office, 1972–4. Leading member of the 'Suez Group' of Conservative MPs.

SIR JOHN BIGGS-DAVISON MP Vice-chairman of the Conservative Party Foreign and Commonwealth Affairs Committee and front bench spokesman on foreign affairs.

LORD BLAKE Provost of The Queen's College, Oxford since 1968. Author of *The Unknown PM – the Life of Bonar Law* (1955), *Disraeli* (1966) and *A History of Rhodesia* (1977).

ROELOF FREDERIK (PIK) BOTHA South African Minister of Foreign Affairs since 1977. Born 1932. Joined the South African Department of Foreign Affairs in 1953. Served with diplomatic missions in Europe 1955–66 and as legal adviser to the Department of Foreign Affairs in 1966–8. Was Under Secretary for Foreign Affairs 1968–70. Ambassador and Permanent Representative of South Africa at the United Nations 1974–7; Ambassador to the USA 1975–7.

RT HON. LORD CARRINGTON MP First Lord of the Admiralty 1959–63; Defence Secretary 1970–4; Foreign Secretary 1979–82.

JOAQUIM CHISSANO Born 1939 in Chibuto, Mozambique. Assistant Secretary to the President of FRELIMO in charge of education 1963–6; Secretary to President of FRELIMO 1966–9; Chief Representative of FRELIMO in Dar es Salaam 1969–74; Foreign Minister of Mozambique, then President following the death of Samora Machel in 1986.

RT HON. SIR IAN GILMOUR MP Lord Privy Seal and Foreign Minister 1979–81.

IAN GOW MP Parliamentary Private Secretary to the Prime Minister 1979–83.

AIR VICE-MARSHAL HAROLD HAWKINS Commander of the Rhodesian Air Force at the time of the Unilateral Declaration of Independence.

ROBERT JACKSON MP Member of Lord Soames's Cabinet at the European Commission in Brussels, 1974–6; Special Assistant to Lord Soames as Governor of Rhodesia 1979–80.

DAVID KENNETH KAUNDA President of Zambia since October 1964. Born 1924; taught at Munali Secondary School 1943–4, where he was headmaster 1944–8; boarding master, Mufulira Upper School 1948–9; District Secretary, African National Congress, 1950–2; Provincial Organizing Secretary 1952–3 and Secretary-General, 1953–8. National President of the Zambia African National Congress 1958–9; President of the United National Independence Party 1960; Chairman of the Pan-African Freedom Movement for East, Central and Southern Africa, 1962. Minister of Local Government, Northern Rhodesia, 1962–3; Prime Minister of Northern Rhodesia, January–October 1964. Chairman of the Organization of African Unity, 1970 and of the non-aligned countries also in 1970.

ROBERT MUGABE Born at Kutama Mission 1924, where he received his early education from Jesuits. Later educated at University of Fort Hare, South Africa; BA 1951. Elected Secretary General of ZANU 1963. Arrested and detained 1963–74. Leader of ZANU at the Lancaster House Conference, September–December 1979. Prime Minister of Zimbabwe–Rhodesia 1980 and President of Zimbabwe from 1980.

BISHOP ABEL MUZOREWA Prime Minister of Rhodesia under Ian Smith's 'internal settlement', 1979.

JOSHUA NKOMO Born in Bulawayo 1917; educated Adams College, Natal, and University of South Africa. Organizing Secretary, Rhodesian Railways Union 1945–50. President of the African National Congress 1957. Imprisoned 1963–4. In detention 1964–74. Leader of ZAPU and joint leader of the Patriotic Front 1976–80.

GENERAL OLUSEGUN OBASANJO Head of the federal military government and commander-in-chief of the armed forces, Nigeria, 1976–9. Member of the Advisory Council of State since 1979.

SIR MICHAEL PALLISER Head of Chancery, Dakar, 1960–2; Counsellor, 1963. Head of Planning Staff at the Foreign Office 1964; Private Secretary to Prime Minister Harold Wilson 1966. Permanent Under Secretary, Foreign and Commonwealth Office, and Head of the Diplomatic Service 1975–82.

ACHILLES SYMEON PAPADOPOULOS, CMG British Ambassador to Mozambique, 1979–80. Previously Ambassador to El Salvador, 1977–9 and member of the UK Mission to the United Nations, 1980.

SIR ANTHONY PARSONS GCMG Deputy Under Secretary of the Foreign Office supervising Rhodesia policy in 1979. UK Permanent Representative to the United Nations 1979–82; special adviser to the Prime Minister on Foreign Affairs, 1982–3.

SIR SHRIDATH 'SONNY' RAMPHAL Commonwealth Secretary General.

IAN DOUGLAS SMITH Prime Minister of Rhodesia from April 1964 to November 1965 when the Unilateral Declaration of Independence was made. Thereafter leader of the rebel Rhodesia Front government.

I

Chance, Change and Margaret Thatcher

The British are woven with their long and continuous history. An enduring whisper of that history has been Mary Tudor's lament at the loss of England's last possession on the continent of Europe, a symbol of the power and primacy of medieval England which bit deeply into heart and conscience: 'When I am dead and opened you shall find "Calais" lying in my heart.'[1] Queen Mary bore witness that the process of withdrawal and return from the great engagements of empire is unpleasantly remembered, and invariably painful. The British have been called upon to perform the task twice – in the return from empire in France and, over the last forty years, in the return from the wider empire overseas. Among those things buried in the mind of the British as a nation state is the difficulty, at the end of the day, in giving up 'The Last Possession'.

So it was with Rhodesia, the last colony in Africa. As in the time of the Tudors, ministers were embarked on profound reform and retrenchment. The difference was that, this time, Britain was returning not to the status of an island power moored off the continent, but once more to the integrated life of Europe from which it had withdrawn under the Tudors. The divisive issue of 'Europe' hastened a progressive turning away from the past, from the great colonial achievement, from the Pax Britannica of Cecil Rhodes's dreams and from his life-long belief in the superiority of the Anglo-Saxon race. The future of Rhodesia, imbued with emotions about British 'kith and kin' and a certain view of Britain in the world, became one of the most exacting assignments in all the repertory of diplomacy.

1 Holinshed, *Chronicles*, iii.1160. Calais was an English possession from 1347 to 1558.

From the outset, Ian Smith's rebellion was a gamble inviting retribution. The situation of land-locked Rhodesia violated the two major canons of imperial security: 'Never be out of reach of the Royal Navy, or the Indian Army.' Change and choice had placed Rhodesia beyond the arm of both. Successive British governments had expended themselves on many an appeal and pilgrimage to the heart of Africa, to no avail. Around the walls of Ian Smith's Jericho many trumpets had been blown, among them Henry Kissinger's, whose 'shuttle diplomacy' has been described as 'an infinite capacity for taking planes'.[2] By 1979, however, Ian Smith and the embattled diehards of the Rhodesia Front were lonely men waiting for the tide to play upon the sandcastles. The ultimate defection from his cause, that of South Africa, had finally forced **Ian Smith** to accept the principle of black majority rule.

It was not a decision that we welcomed, or that we accepted lightly, I must tell you that. We were placed in a situation where we virtually had no option. This was because of the actions of the then South African Prime Minister, John Vorster. As far as countries like Britain and America were concerned, we could defy them as we had done over the years. We could not do that to the one country which controlled our life-line. So, reluctantly – *very* reluctantly – we were forced to accept it.

We believed that, if we had been given more time, we would have been more successful. We would have liked to continue with our philosophy, which was one of meritocracy as opposed to accepting the philosophy of 'one man, one vote', which I have always condemned. I have likened it to the counting of sheep. I believe that a system which says that your most competent, most intelligent, most principled man only has the same say in the government of his country as your most *in*competent, *un*intelligent, *un*principled man is madness. I go further, and say, that while that might apply specifically to Africa – where people have never participated in the democratic system – I have a feeling that in countries such as Britain, and the United States of America, that if *you* had a kind of meritocracy, you would have better governments than you have today.

Very little of what happened between you and Kissinger and Vorster in 1976

2 Henry Kissinger was US Secretary of State under Presidents Nixon and Ford, 1973–7. The term 'shuttle diplomacy' was coined to describe his diplomatic activity in ending the 1973 Arab–Israeli war. Kissinger's two visits to Africa were made in 1976.

has been revealed.[3] *I think you've just confirmed that it was inconceivable, had it not been for Vorster's arm-twisting, that you would have agreed to black majority rule: you, the man who had said 'never in a thousand years', suddenly accept it. What really happened?*

Contrary to what many people think, Kissinger was very fair with us. He made it clear that the agreement he was selling was not his, or an American, agreement. I knew that the Americans did not know enough about us, or our problems to produce that. It was a British agreement. About half-way through our discussions, some complicated problem came up and I gave him information of which he was unaware. We broke, so that they could go outside and consult with the British ambassador. In fact a telephone call was put right through to London. So we knew, and Kissinger conceded, that it was a *British* agreement.

I was surprised how reasonable he was over the whole affair. He put his cards on the table with complete honesty. He told me that that *was* the agreement and, regrettably, that there was no negotiation on it because it had already been accepted by a number of the other major European powers. It had been accepted by the leaders in black Africa, particularly Nyerere,[4] who had said he would support it. And so, 'Regrettably,' Kissinger said to me, 'I can only offer you this. And, if you turn it down,' he said, 'I want to assure you there will be no recrimination as far as I am concerned. Only you can make the decision. It is your country and your lives at stake.'

After that we went up to the Prime Minister's residence in Pretoria, 'Libertas'.[5] That is where the pressure was *really* applied to us. As a matter of interest it was the first time in my life I had seen Pik Botha,[6] and I wondered who he was! Jack Gaylard, then the Secretary of our Cabinet, had to tell me. He was then the South African ambassador in America. There was a lot of talk. It went on for hours and hours. It is difficult to summarize everything but, in the end, we got the message from the South African Prime Minister. The South Africans had come to the conclusion that we had no option. We *had* to accept this agreement. So, that was it.

Only South Africa, not Kissinger, not anybody else, only *South Africa had the power to force you to change your mind and it is this threat that made you do so. But what was the threat?*

3 This meeting between Kissinger and Smith was in September 1976. Together with Kissinger's previous visit in April the same year, it led ultimately to the 'internal settlement' with Bishop Muzorewa in 1979.

4 President Julius Nyerere of Tanzania.

5 The residence of Prime Minister Vorster of South Africa.

6 Now South Africa's Foreign Minister.

It was very simple. They controlled our lines of communication, our supplies. Where else could we obtain our supplies, other than from South Africa? And we were assured that we had to accept this, otherwise the South Africans would not be able to go on playing their part.

How was that put to you?

I don't want to be too personal. I've told you, quite clearly, we got the message that South Africa had come to the conclusion we must accept. Vorster didn't say, 'If you don't I'll chop your head off,' but that message was clear and unequivocal, and we knew from experience that this was very real.

Will history be right to suggest that you ignored the underlying reality that South Africa would not *support white Rhodesia at all costs?*

We gave this matter very serious consideration. I did not make the decision then and there. I had three of my colleagues with me. We flew back to Salisbury that very evening and next day had a meeting with my Cabinet. It was a unanimous conclusion. We had no option.

The point where you misjudged South Africa, fundamentally, I suggest, is this. Black majority rule here in Rhodesia did not alarm South Africa. The South Africans took the view that if white Rhodesians had wanted South African support then that opportunity had been passed up as early as 1923.[7]

I don't believe that that really was of any consequence. The people with whom we were talking were not part of that history. What changed the South African position was the new philosophy the South African Prime Minister had espoused, one of 'détente'. That was something completely new. He was of the opinion that he could work with the black leaders to the north of us, and help to solve the Rhodesian problem. He told me this. In return, the black countries to the north were going to accept South Africa and their philosophy. So to a certain extent we were to be used as a sacrificial lamb in helping to solve *South Africa*'s problem. I did not believe that it would work. My remarks to the South African Prime Minister, I still remember, very clearly, were: 'If in the final analysis Rhodesia has to be used, in this way, to save South Africa, that would be *one* thing. But, as I understand it, of course it is *not* going to save South Africa. So we are making the sacrifice for nothing.' That was a major point on which we disagreed. He just believed that his contact with the black leaders to

7 When rule by the British South Africa Company ended and Rhodesia became a self-governing colony, annexed to the Crown.

the north of us was something I was unaware of and did not understand. Well, I've lived in Africa all my life and although I wasn't present at the meetings, I think I have a very good understanding of black Africa and black leaders in Africa. And history proves that I was right, and he was wrong.

Ian Smith, the Smith of Smiths, is there assuming the mantle he so often wore, the mantle of the outcast, cast out because he had to speak the truth. But his truth was one that could not be made a matter of practical politics.

Following Mr Vorster's virtual ultimatum, in 1976, Rhodesia's white minority[8] began to bid a more palpable farewell to a heyday irrevocably passing. Even so, nothing seemed more intractable, more perplexing and more seemingly insoluble than the question of Rhodesia.

In 1979, three weeks before the Conservatives led by Margaret Thatcher came to power in Britain, Ian Smith had held elections in Rhodesia which returned a predominantly black government. It was led by Bishop Abel Muzorewa, who thus became Rhodesia's first black Prime Minister. The question for Britain was whether to recognize this government and grant to it legal independence, which would in turn win a sufficient international recognition.

On his first morning as the new Foreign Secretary, Lord Carrington had announced to his senior Foreign Office officials: 'We're going to settle it.' But while there was a feeling that 'things could not go on like this', there was no clear idea of how or where resolution was to come. Carrington began his diplomacy as the bush war in Rhodesia intensified; it was attended by great suspicion in his own party, and indeed among all parties to the dispute.

Lord Carrington was at the height of his powers in the job he had always wanted. He had long experience in the conduct of defence and strategic policy. If his career had not always been attended by the kind of monotonous success Sir Lancelot enjoyed, nevertheless he had an effortless style and charm that seemed to rise serenely above difficulty. He refused to be drawn into melodrama, and all in all he seemed the very embodiment of the diplomatist's maxim 'where there's a will there's a way round.' He came to office in 1979 undoubtedly intolerant of the immoderate degree of attention the Rhodesian issue continued to exact from British politics, and the futility of the colonial mythology which clung to it.

Immediately before his return to office as Foreign Secretary in

8 A quarter of a million whites in a population of 3 million, at the time of UDI in 1965.

Margaret Thatcher's first Conservative government, **Lord Carrington** had been on the boards of two great companies with their roots in the British imperial period in southern Africa: Barclays Bank and the mining conglomerate, Rio Tinto Zinc. This experience was important in concentrating his mind.

It was one of the reasons why I gratefully accepted the invitation to join these two companies. Because it did give me the opportunity of getting there, and making a judgement. I had always been interested in foreign affairs and wanted to know more about that part of the world. The judgement I came to was that time was running out in Rhodesia, and that it was in the British interest to try and get it settled, if possible, on a basis agreed by everybody. That was not a particularly dramatic conclusion, because that was what *all* British governments had been trying to do for quite a long time. But I thought time was running out.

How did you assess the vital interest of raw materials in this part of the world to Britain, a member, by this time, of the European Community?

There were some who said it was important that the South African regime should go on, and that the Rhodesian regime should go on, because there were so many important minerals there. I confess, I never thought that was a very powerful argument. It has always seemed to me that the economic necessities of those countries were such that it would be necessary for them to sell minerals. I did not think it was very likely that they were going to be cut off. There were those who suggested that the Soviet Union would intervene. There was no doubt that, at that time, the Soviet ambassador in Lusaka was really the head of a sort of network which was trying to promote Soviet interests in that part of the world. But even given that, it did not seem to me that the Soviet Union was very likely to be in a position to control whether the minerals from southern Africa were exported. I don't think that was a very important issue. Of course it was important to the companies concerned but not, I think, nationally.

From what perspective did you take this overall position? How far were you governed by the opinion that – because, originally, our colonization of the Cape had been to secure the passage to India – Britain having quit India, all that was over?

That's right. It would be difficult to visualize the passage around the Cape, in current circumstances, or in the circumstances at that time, as being a vital strategic interest. Of course, you could think up situations in which it *would* be very important. But, after all, I had

> spent quite a lot of my career either in Defence or at the Admiralty, and I have never been convinced that, in any future war, the route around the Cape is likely to be of really vital interest to the West.

Rhodesia was thus reduced to the status of a highly charged but largely emotional issue. What then were the roots of British policy by 1979? Lord Carrington's judgement that the time had come to settle the Rhodesian question was powerfully supported by Foreign Office advice. The new government had come to power with a totally disillusioned attitude towards the value of mandatory sanctions.[9] As a form of coercion it was regarded as a failure, and its continuation, now that Ian Smith had bent the knee to the principle of black majority rule, was fiercely divisive of the Conservative Party. The turnout at the elections Smith had held in Rhodesia in April 1979 had been impressive. Pressures were mounting on the new government to give Rhodesia independence and lift sanctions forthwith. The awesome logic was that if ministers were not prepared to lift sanctions, then they had to get a settlement, and the widest recognition of it, as soon as possible.

Faced with Rhodesia's daunting realities, joyous imagination had deserted the Foreign Office; a solution had eluded the efforts of successive governments over many years, and the situation had worsened after each attempt. A generation of officials had wearied of the question beyond pleasure. By 1979, most of the time of the Foreign and Commonwealth Office, was being taken up by the need constantly to explain and defend this aspect of British policy before the world.

The head of the Foreign Office as Mrs Thatcher's government took office was **Sir Michael Palliser**.

> One can say that you get used to that. To take a different example, it still goes on once a year at the United Nations over the Falklands. But Rhodesia was more intense, and more acute. I'm not sure that was a determinant so much as the momentum that had been generated, towards a negotiated settlement, throughout all the period of the Labour government, under David Owen.[10] There was a feeling that there *had* to be a negotiated settlement of this problem. It wasn't something that one could just see as an annual, continuing irritant in our relations at the United Nations and with African countries. I think there was a feeling that enough had been done – although it had not produced a result – to have created a situation. Either you went

9 Following UDI, selective mandatory sanctions were applied against Rhodesia by the United Nations at the end of 1966.
10 Foreign Secretary in James Callaghan's government, 1977–9.

forward with the negotiation, in whatever shape or form, to reach a settlement or things would get worse and just decline. It was not just a question of our relations at the UN, or with countries in Africa, but it was something that was going to cause us a great deal of trouble if it was *not* resolved.

Should we be in any doubt that the underlying feeling in the Foreign Office was that we had *to extricate ourselves from Rhodesia, we had to 'get shot' of the Rhodesian problem?*

No. I think that's fair.

As the Conservatives came to power in 1979, at your first meetings with the new Foreign Secretary, in what terms did he talk of the need, as opposed to the wish, to get a settlement in Rhodesia?

I certainly remember two things. One was during the election campaign, when he was being interviewed with Owen on TV. The interviewer was doing his utmost to persuade them to disagree with each other about the need for a settlement in Rhodesia and the kind of settlement there should be, and he failed. I was impressed by this during the campaign. It seemed to me that if Lord Carrington was going to be Foreign Secretary, as most of us expected him to be, there would no doubt be a very different method of *handling* things, but the broad political approach did not strike me as very different. Then, of course, when he spoke to me after the election, on the Friday morning, to tell me he was being appointed Foreign Secretary, obviously Rhodesia was one of the principal subjects. It was clear to me, from the discussion he had with me then, that his general approach was going to be towards a negotiated settlement, and an orderly and responsible disengagement from Rhodesia.

Was his idea of a negotiated settlement qualified in any important way? Was it to secure in Rhodesia a moderate and pro-Western government, or was it simply to settle *it?*

Obviously, ideally, the former. What that meant in practical terms, and who should be in that government, we were not discussing at that stage. I think you have got to remember that, then, Robert Mugabe himself was very little known. Now he has become a world figure, certainly a very significant African figure, but *then* he was basically a guerrilla leader, operating in the bush. Nobody really had any idea of what his approach would be. Interestingly, he was seen as that part of the guerrilla leadership that had problems with Moscow, and depended more for support on Peking, whereas one of the criticisms that had regularly been made of Joshua Nkomo was that *he* relied too heavily on support from the Soviet Union. I think both those judgements were overplayed. But it is quite interesting now, looking back, to think that Mugabe was *not* seen as a sort of Soviet instrument.

Therefore, we had an objective beyond any immediate settlement. It was to limit the expanding Russian influence in that part of the world. In which case, even though Mugabe himself was avowedly a Marxist–Leninist, you were inclined to discount that because of his 'difficult' relationship with the Russians?

Yes, I think we were. It is probably true that a certain number of the incoming Conservative government in 1979 did, indeed, believe in the expansion of Russian influence in Africa. And some people in the Foreign Office did. I, personally, partly from my own time in Africa but more generally because of the interest I've had in Africa for many years, was much more sceptical about that. It seemed to me that every time the Russians got involved in Africa they tended to make a mess of it. Take Ethiopia. At that time it looked as if their presence in Ethiopia was indeed going to be very sinister, and dangerous. Ethiopia is now a matter of human tragedy[11] but I do not think anybody sees it as a driving force for communism throughout Africa. Then, another eight or ten years further on, take Angola, and the presence of the Cubans. It is not clear to me that that has produced, other than in Angola itself, any substantial expansion of Russian influence. It is an interesting paradox that Mozambique, which was regarded as a very Marxist and Soviet-influenced country, played the most helpful part, in due course, towards a settlement in Rhodesia: I do not think for Russian purposes.

However, the Soviet ambassador to Zambia, in Lusaka, Ambassador Salodnikov, was understood to be a full KGB[12] General and, as Lord Carrington says, 'at the head of a sort of network trying to promote Soviet interests in that part of the world.' You agree that that was a consideration in the choice of Mugabe, who did not enjoy his patronage?

Yes. I do. But I do not say 'the choice of Mugabe'. No one 'chose' Mugabe. He was the chosen leader of his tribe[13] and of that segment of black Rhodesian opinion. It is perfectly true that the Russians were extremely active. But it is one thing to be active, another to be successful. I have always been sceptical about the measure of their success in their penetration of Africa.

11 A reference to the warfare, drought and famine suffered by Ethiopia in the 1980s.

12 Soviet Committee of State Security.

13 The Mashona.

by this time had moved out of empire, found 'Commonwealth' ...icient, and joined the European Community. What did the Foreign ...ce consider was the importance of southern Africa, as a whole?

...ou have to divide it into three parts: politics, economics and security. I confess myself to having always been a bit sceptical about the importance of southern Africa in terms of security. That goes back to the days of the Simonstown base.[14] I'm not suggesting, for a moment, that I would wish to see a Soviet base at Simonstown, or a Soviet presence in South Africa, but it always seemed to me to be a mistake to see South Africa, under the system that has prevailed there for a number of years, as a bastion of Western security. If anything, it is a bastion of Western *insecurity*. Which leaves politics and economics. Economically, there is no doubt at all about the importance of South Africa. Investments and raw materials add up to a very significant Western interest. It was certainly seen as very powerfully the case, ten years ago, that a certain number of raw materials came only from either South Africa or the Soviet Union. If one is talking of southern Africa, therefore, one is looking at it, essentially, in a political context – the economic importance of South Africa, South West Africa and Namibia.

Inevitably South Africa and Rhodesia were linked economically. We had accepted economic sanctions against Rhodesia while recognizing that, as long as the frontier with South Africa was open, their impact was bound to be limited. But the political or moral pressure was so great that it was inevitable that economic sanctions against Rhodesia should be accepted. Also, Rhodesia was much smaller. You have got to remember that Rhodesia is a sort of village, in terms of a white population, compared with South Africa. Rhodesia was seen as a much smaller target. However, as long as South Africa was prepared to sustain Rhodesia, economic sanctions were bound to be pretty ineffective.

Is it not of interest that the two oldest nation states in Europe, Britain and France, came to different conclusions about the importance of Africa? France supports black governments within the French Union, or Community, with military guarantees against all manner of disturbance. In that sense, France has 'stayed on' in Africa, while Britain continued to withdraw, and the machinery of de-colonization continued to operate, right down to the

14 Near Cape Town. In 1967 Britain abolished the post of Commander-in-Chief South Atlantic. In 1974, following re-imposition of an arms embargo, Prime Minister Wilson told South Africa that Britain no longer regarded the Simonstown agreement as operative.

Rhodesian settlement. What explanation for that would you encourage historians of the future to accept?

That is a fascinating subject which one could discuss for a very long time! First of all, by the time of 'de-colonization', virtually the only colonial properties that France owned were in Africa. There were possessions in the Caribbean; it is having a little bit of trouble in the Pacific at the moment;[15] and of course France is still very actively involved on the continent of Latin America, with its rocket-launching achievements in French Guiana. But, fundamentally, France's colonial empire was African. The other interesting thing about the French empire was that, with one or two exceptions, on the whole the French had got the *poorest* bits of Africa. The British, before the 1914–18 war, and subsequently with the dismantling of the German colonial empire, had got the richest bits. Partly because they *were* the richest bits, I think they were the most independently minded. Ghana is now in rather sad economic condition, although improving. But if you think back to 1957, Ghana was a kind of economic jewel, with the largest cocoa exports in the world. Nigeria was a giant which had hardly been born in economic terms but was obviously of enormous potential. Kenya was prosperous. Nigeria and Kenya were the two, east and west, African jewels of the former British colonial crown. Given that situation, the French made the utmost of their bits of Africa. To my mind, the most significant feature of the continuing French strength in Africa is not the military treaties, which are a bit of an encumbrance in some ways, but the fact of the continuing control of the currencies by France, through the franc zone. The fact is that whether it is the Ivory Coast, or Senegal, or any of the other Francophone countries and former colonies, they are still run, financially, from Paris. That has been a great advantage to them. And it has been of considerable commercial and economic advantage to France! Now, as for us, the sterling area no longer exists. We had run our colonies quite differently and we *de*-colonized in accordance with that. It meant that when one visited the Gambia, as I used to do, from Senegal, in the early 1960s, one found this extraordinarily impoverished little country, where the Governor was the only person in the colony who had an air conditioner in his bedroom because the colony had to pay for itself, and it had not got much to pay with! Nigeria was a very different proposition because *it* had lots to pay with in those days. That is the way we ran our empire. The French did not do that. They ran it in typical French fashion. They centralized

15 I.e. rebellion in New Caledonia.

from Paris and they continue to centralize from Paris, and good luck to them. I think it has been beneficial to those African countries that played the game. Guinea is the exception that proved the rule and it has begun to come back to the fold anyway.

Had something like the French connection been considered thoughtfully by us, before we made up our minds to get out of Africa, and Macmillan made his speech about 'the wind of change',[16] *or again before we took the final plunge?*

No. Even if it had been considered it would not have been possible. We could not have controlled the Nigerian currency from London. We were not prepared to put troops into Nigeria or to keep troops in Nigeria, because the Nigerians did not want us to; I just take those as examples. These were not options.

'We're going to settle it', Lord Carrington had said that first morning in office to his Foreign Office advisers, and it had the ring of 'once and for all' about it. It also meant that neither he, nor they, were persuaded that Ian Smith's achievement, immediately before the British general election in 1979, of a government in which blacks predominated, could endure.

In the Conservative Party there were formidable opponents, rather than a formidable opposition, to the Foreign Office advice and Lord Carrington's judgement that Smith's internal settlement did not go far enough. They were among Margaret Thatcher's most ardent supporters. The Suez Group[17] of MPs had been formed at the time of the Suez debacle in 1956 when, as Eden was forced to capitulate, the party almost fell apart. It embodied sentiments which had proved lethal to one Conservative leader, Eden, and it had remained a thorn in Macmillan's flesh throughout his Prime Ministership, opposing every step in the dissolution of the African empire. Its members were vigilant opponents of any disposition to feebleness in foreign policy, of any weakness in the face of American pressure and, particularly, of anything that smacked of tame servitude to 'Third World' demands. In 1979, believing that the principles[18] laid down by Britain for Rhodesia's legal independence had now been met by Salisbury, these influential Conservatives were pressing for recognition of Ian Smith's multi-racial government, led by Bishop

16 Delivered before the South African parliament in Cape Town, 3 February 1960.

17 Led by Captain Charles Waterhouse and Julian Amery.

18 The fifth principle, and the key element, was that 'the basis for a settlement should be acceptable to the people of Rhodesia as a whole.'

Abel Muzorewa, over the claims of the Patriotic Front and its leaders, Robert Mugabe and Joshua Nkomo, who were waging war against it.

A conspicuous member of the Suez Group, as the bearer of a name resonant in imperial affairs, was Julian Amery, the son of the empire statesman Leo Amery.[19] In opposing Lord Carrington, and the settlement which was finally to be reached at Lancaster House, did **Julian Amery** consider that the two hundred thousand white Rhodesians had a permanent claim on British loyalty?

I don't think they had a permanent claim on our *loyalty*, but they had a permanent claim on our *understanding*. We had interests of a very important character. To neglect those interests, in favour of a *theory*, was wrong. Always, there is this argument that there is an 'inevitability' about majority rule. My own reading of history over the last forty-five years does not convince me that that is so. Most of the countries in the world, or at least a great number of them, are not ruled by the majorities, or by democracy. Rhodesia was almost a full dominion before Smith proclaimed his UDI in 1965, and there was a long history of the British government not intervening in Rhodesian affairs. I think Smith made a mistake in declaring UDI. Had he *waited* for the British government to try to interfere, he would have been on impregnable ground in turning them down, and going ahead as if he *were* independent. He did not do that. So, the Wilson government over-reacted, in my view, in trying to bring down a government which was 90 per cent independent before UDI. It became clear that the Wilson government could not use force. It would not have got British armed forces to do it.

Does that mean you think there would have been another 'Curragh'?[20]

Yes, I think so. I remember an earlier phase, when the Central African Federation[21] was breaking up. I was in a Service Department at the time. One of the Chiefs of Staff came to see me to say that the Colonial Secretary had asked the Chiefs of Staff to prepare a contingency plan for invading. This Chief of Staff said to me, 'I think

19 Leo Amery (1873–1955) was a foremost advocate of a united Commonwealth and empire. He was Colonial and Dominions Secretary 1924–9 and Secretary of State for India and Burma 1940 and 1945.

20 In March 1914 British army officers at the Curragh Camp, Dublin, threatened resignation rather than be used in the military coercion of Ulster into accepting Home Rule. Often known as the 'Curragh Mutiny'.

21 Federation formed in September 1953, comprising the British central African territories of Southern Rhodesia (now Zimbabwe), Northern Rhodesia (now Zambia) and Nyasaland (now Malawi). Finally dissolved in December 1963.

this is very dangerous indeed. I do hope you can interfere.' I said, 'Well, I'm all against it, but isn't it fairly normal to make contingency plans?' He said, 'You must realize that we've got Rhodesian officers on the Planning Staff.' So I picked up the telephone to Downing Street and killed it.

Did you have a concept of nation, or of the unity of national sentiment, in which Rhodesia played a part?

Yes, and I think that is often forgotten. There were some two hundred thousand people of British origin in Rhodesia, and in South Africa there were two million of British origin. Think what that means in terms of their relations – people in this country who have a personal link with Rhodesia. On top of that, there were those who had a business link of some kind. We thought it amounted to well over ten million people in Britain who were, in one way or another, directly linked with southern Africa. What Wilson was trying to do, if it had led to the collapse of what you might call 'civilized government' in Rhodesia, would obviously alienate them. I toured the country speaking on the subject. There was very little anti-Rhodesian sentiment, at any rate in the early stages, outside the 'chattering classes'. It grew a certain amount, on the Labour side, when the civil war became more marked. But that did not happen until 1975.

But what you were calling for in Rhodesia went against the grain, would you agree, of British prejudices at that time?

Not of the prejudices of the broad mass of our people. On the contrary, if you'd had a referendum, you would have had very strong support, probably majority support, for the line that I was taking. That was, 'no sanctions against Rhodesia'.

Therefore you are saying – what? This is a failure of the political class in Britain?

Yes, certainly. In my view, the political class has been failing since the beginning of the century, after which we began to turn our backs. We had moments of revival; the Lloyd George government struck very much the right note, during the second half of the First World War; there was the Ottawa Conference;[22] and the Churchill government. But there has been an element of *trahison des clercs*, if you like, in a large section of the political class.

22 The imperial economic conference in 1932, at which the dominions lowered tariffs on British manufactures and Britain admitted dominion produce free of duty. It marked Britain's abandonment of its traditional free trade policy.

How would you describe the nature of that failure?

Firstly, very large economic losses – most evident, at the moment, in South Africa – but Rhodesia was an enormous treasure house. Our investments in Rhodesia have all gone, or are frozen and pretty well valueless.

A loss of influence. The French have been wiser than we have, although it has cost them a lot of money. While playing a leading part in Europe they've managed also to play a neo-imperial role. *We* have lost, and *they* dominate west Africa. Of course, the French empire was, essentially, a west African *black* empire, but they decided to keep as much as they could and by indirect methods they've succeeded. The French gave independence, quicker than we did, to all their African colonies. But they so managed the retreat from empire that they were able to leave garrisons behind and civil servants behind, albeit at high cost. When we gave independence to the mass of our colonies we were pushed into a new position where South Africa was concerned. All governments, Labour as well as Conservative, were very strong in their support for South Africa, at the United Nations and elsewhere, *until* we gave independence to the black countries. Once we did that, the desire to maintain, or improve, relations with them led us into increasingly strident criticism of South Africa and into taking up the racist issue.

Did not our historical relationship with the United States, the degree to which we accepted the universality of the American Revolution, foreclose the possibility of doing other than we did, or as the French had done in Africa? There was the ending of 'separate but equal' in the Southern states of America, and then the great civil rights movement of the 1960s. One man, one vote?

I think we could have stood against it. The question is, were we justified, and I think we were *not*, in trying to impose what you might call American civil rights standards on Rhodesia and South Africa. We should have let them evolve, in their own way.

Would you agree, as a member of the Suez Group, which was formed after Anthony Eden had resolved to quit the Suez base in 1954, that this notion of 'giving way', of 'capitulation', is a recurring theme of your interventions? To what extent was 'capitulation' dramatized for you in the choice Britain had to make over Rhodesia?

For once it was not 'giving way', in the classical sense, because we were not *there.* It was a question of whether we should use British resources to compel other countries, in this case Rhodesia – and, by extension, South Africa – to behave differently from how they wanted to. This was a form of neo-colonialism. We wanted to dictate to them *how* they should evolve. It was 'capitulation' only in the sense that it was the abandonment of important British interests. But, yes, the philosophy *behind* it was the philosophy that had led us to capitulation. Having accepted the principle of capitulation with 'the wind of change', we went beyond that. Having thrown away the card, we tried to dictate how the future should develop.

However, that would have meant an alteration in the whole stance from which British political thinking was being conducted.

I don't think so. We were not, in those days, telling Dr Salazar,[23] or General Franco,[24] how to run their countries. We had perfectly good relations with them, *and* trade, and we kept out of interfering in their domestic affairs. The same is true with a great many other dictatorships, whether we liked them or didn't like them. There was an element of shock or revulsion at the declaration of UDI; and provoked by the declaration of UDI, technically a dangerous step which led to a breach with the Crown, we then went on the offensive. It was neo-imperialism. That was the basis of my attitude in saying to Wilson, 'I think you've over-reacted. It is a mistake to put on sanctions and a terrible mistake to put on *mandatory* sanctions.' It was even more of a mistake because it could not succeed. It was not the sanctions that brought about the Lancaster House talks,[25] it was the nature of the civil war; and that did not develop until the early 1970s, after the Portuguese Revolution. So, I saw it as a foolish policy. In some ways it was reminiscent of the attitude of George the Third and Lord North[26] toward George Washington. There again, the British government of the day, Lord North's government, made much of the racial discrimination practised against the Red Indians in North America by the Washington government. There is a certain parallel there.

You would share the view that Lord North was the worst Prime Minister we have had?[27]

23 Prime Minister and dictator in Portugal from 1932 to 1968.

24 Spanish head of state 1938–75.

25 The talks convened at Lancaster House, London, where the fate of so many of Britain's former colonies had been decided, from 10 September to 21 December 1979, and where provision was made for the cease-fire and elections (see chapters 4–6).

26 Prime Minister and First Lord of the Treasury 1770–82.

27 The calamitous loss of Britain's thirteen American colonies in 1783 after the War of Independence that began in 1776 prompted Horace Walpole to say, 'The best that can be allotted to Lord North is that, though his country was ruined under his administration he preserved his good humour' (G. F. R. Barker, ed., *Memoirs of the Reign of George the Third* (London, 1894), vol. IV, p. 55).

Yes. Always a case to be made for anyone, of course. Up to a point.

For the Suez Group, the Munich analogy, 'appeasement', was a dominant one. 'Munich' was much spoken of in considering what to do about Colonel Nasser.[28] *Did you take the view it was the same sentiment, when it came to Carrington, that he was 'appeasing' the Patriotic Front?*

In a sense it's worse, isn't it? Neville Chamberlain and Anthony Eden were appeasing an *enemy*, or an adversary, of Britain. It was arguable, from their point of view, that this was a gamble that might pay off. What we did at Lancaster House was not to appease, but to turn round and punish *ourselves*. It was a masochistic exercise.

Julian Amery deplored a diplomacy which ended, he believed, by supporting adversaries of the British interest to destroy the *primacy* of that interest.

Ninety years before, Rhodesia had been acquired, together with Kenya, Nigeria and Uganda, during the stewardship over foreign policy of the third Lord Salisbury.[29] Salisbury was a Conservative Prime Minister of intellectual authority, with an almost Aristotelian fear of democracy as mob rule, and certainly of any unqualified democratization of thought and ideas.[30] None the less, Salisbury had held that the central doctrine of Conservatism should be that 'it was better to endorse almost any political evil rather than risk the historic continuity of government.' Was this not at heart Lord Carrington's approach? In which case, given that Britain held responsibility where Rhodesia was concerned, but was without real power, why was a thoughtful Conservative like **Sir John Biggs-Davison**, another member of the Suez Group, unwilling to endorse it?

There was a feeling that the Southern Rhodesians had been shamefully treated. In 1961 they were assured that, if they accepted the Sandys[31] constitution, they would not be required to enter into more concessions. That constitution was intended to produce majority rule through the educational and economic advancement of the Africans. Incidentally, the black nationalist leaders at that time, Mr Sithole and Mr Nkomo,

28 President of Egypt from 1956, and of the United Arab Republic from 1958 until his death on 28 September 1970.

29 British Prime Minister 1885, 1886–92 and 1895–1900.

30 He is still remembered for having described the new popular journalism of the *Daily Mail* as 'by office boys, for office boys'.

31 Duncan Sandys, Secretary of State for Commonwealth Relations, July 1960–October 1964.

after first accepting that constitution in London, rejected it when they got home.[32] But the home government continued to deny Rhodesia independence. In 1979, the Conservative Party had a manifesto. That manifesto encouraged the hopes of the Rhodesians and the Conservatives. It said that, if the famous six principles were satisfied, following the British general election in 1979, the incoming government would return Rhodesia to legality, remove sanctions, and do its utmost to obtain recognition for the new independent state. That was a clear assurance.

Lord Carrington wanted to sacrifice obligations that had been entered into, and the manifesto commitment, to the wider consideration of relations with Commonwealth countries and allies. The question arises, was it possible to withstand these pressures without undue loss of British interest? That is a very important question. I think it *was* possible. If the British government had said: 'We have these commitments. We now have an inter-racial government in Southern Rhodesia, which has satisfied the six principles, and which has been endorsed by the people of Rhodesia as a whole. We now propose to recognize this regime, we propose to declare it legal, and it is for us to do so, and for no one else', then, I believe, the situation in southern Africa would have been transformed, because the frontline states[33] were weak, and they were precarious. Rhodesia would have been able to re-equip its forces, and there would have been plenty of people to start trading, and supplying the necessary arms and equipment to the new state.

As you saw it, what was the opportunity when the Conservatives returned to government in May 1979, led by a new Prime Minister, Margaret Thatcher, whose convictions in these matters, one might suppose, were much in sympathy with your own? That, is impatient with the moralizing rectitude of the black states.

And, she had also made a speech in Australia saying she did not think sanctions would be renewed.

Exactly. So what was the opportunity you saw in her leadership?

We hoped for very much from her and we were disappointed when

32 In 1963, Sandys wrote to Winston Field, Smith's predecessor as Rhodesian Prime Minister, 'The present difficulty arises from yr desire to secure independence on a franchise incomparably more restrictive than that of any other British territory to which Independence has hitherto been granted' (from a paper delivered to Harvard University by Sir Robin Renwick, January 1981).

33 Zambia and Mozambique in particular.

she went back on what we had undertaken, in deference to the so-called 'international community', and because of the imminent Commonwealth conference in Lusaka.[34] But, I'm sure you are absolutely right that her opinion and my opinion were identical. Just because of that, it became necessary to Margaret Thatcher that she should get rid of Winston Churchill[35] and me from her front bench. It was because she knew that we were right, or *thought* that we were right, and agreed with us, that it became all the more necessary to insist on complete, and meticulous, loyalty.

How should we see your stand then, in retrospect? Was it the last hurrah of the 'Old Imperialists'?

Who were the 'imperialists'? Was it those who said, as with the American colonies, 'they have established themselves and we should try and make terms with them', or was it the imperialism of those who said to the white Rhodesians, 'You rather inferior suburban people out there must listen to us, and do what we say'?

Lord Salisbury had acknowledged class conflict as a central fact of political life, and he thought that it was irreversible. Did you see what you were advocating as a delaying action, designed to put off, for a little longer, the triumph of the masses in places like southern Africa?

I was concerned not with arresting the advance of the masses in southern Africa, but with the orderly advancement of the territories. Of course, it could not be as slow as would have been ideal, because of what had happened elsewhere in Africa. I remember that, once, Mr Ian Smith was not very pleased with me when I said to him, after UDI, 'Why don't you have some black ministers? *I* could find you some black Africans who'd do the job just as well as some of your white ministers.' So, I was not concerned to prevent the advancement of Africans, I was very much concerned that they should be able to advance, in an orderly manner.

No doubt you recall Mr Smith's reply. What did he say?

I don't think he *said* anything. I think that the temperature of the room fell.

Coldly received in Salisbury, and frozen out of Europe, these were

34 The meeting of Commonwealth heads of government held in Lusaka in August 1979, at which the decision was taken to hold the constitutional conference on Rhodesia which followed at Lancaster House (see chapter 2).

35 Member of Parliament and in 1979 a member of the executive of the Conservative Party '1922 Committee'.

sunless years for the diplomatists charged with shaping the outcome of Britain's complete change of direction. Before the broader trends of historical explanation emerged to win wider acceptance, and human culpability diminished, the Foreign Office remained (for some, indeed, it still is) the object of no little suspicion.

In a celebrated audience which he gave to a British ambassador[36] when Britain was seeking, and denied, membership of the European Community, and was also trying to talk Ian Smith into a settlement, General de Gaulle ran his eyes over the ramparts of Western Europe and gave his opinion concerning that which constituted the 'nation state'. Thus, Germany, now cut in two, was no longer a nation. The poor Italians – always they were '*les pauvres Italiens*' to de Gaulle – had only recently qualified, under Cavour, as a nation. Belgium, the General asserted, 'had been invented by the English in revenge for Napoleon'. Holland? Yes, Holland was a nation but, the General added, 'a very *small* nation'. Which, when all was said, left Britain and France as the only two nation states in Europe to respond to the call of the centuries.

It is from this perspective that historians will surely be interested in why it was that when Britain made the fundamental reappraisal that carried it into Europe, it appeared to take a different view of the importance of black Africa to concepts of nation, and of national unity, than did France. Sir Michael Palliser, as we have seen, considered that 'it is a fascinating subject', while Julian Amery contrasted the will of France, with Britain's beating retreat from southern Africa, in terms of '*We* have lost, and *they* dominate west Africa'. France, under de Gaulle, offered a concrete bridge of direct co-operation, military guarantees and preferential trading between itself and its African territories, and called this 'association'. Independence was deemed to be 'secession', and described as a catastrophe. Those who chose it, like Guinea, were excommunicated and dismissed to the outer darkness. '*Au revoir Guinée*', de Gaulle had pronounced to President Sékou Touré at Conakry[37] with a terrible finality, whereupon France departed from Guinea, taking all the telephones and typewriters with it.

Elsewhere in Africa, France stayed on while Britain's withdrawal was strongly encouraged by official attitudes. Palliser has said that the French connection 'was not an option' for Britain, and the reasons, at a time of such massive adjustments by the British, bear amplifying. As Lord Carrington launched his diplomacy in 1979, among the handful of senior advisers led by Palliser whom he met on the first morning the new

36 Sir Gladwyn Jebb.
37 In August 1958. Charles de Gaulle, *Memoirs of Hope: Renewal and Endeavour* (New York, Simon and Schuster; originally published Paris, Plon, 1970), p. 57.

government took office, when he said to them 'We're going to settle it', was the Deputy Under Secretary of the Foreign Office supervising the Rhodesia policy, **Sir Anthony Parsons**. Parsons had spent almost the whole of a distinguished career involved in the process of de-colonization, both in the real empire and in the 'veiled' empire of the Middle East.

France has always had a very strong cultural dimension to its empire, spreading 'Frenchness' and turning the elite in former colonies into Frenchmen. We have never really taken that view. In our empire we simply accepted what we had found on the spot, tried to make it work as well as possible and, when we had to go away, we went away entirely. We were not trying to project a *mission civilatrice* in our empire. The corollary is that *their* attitude towards the post-imperial epoch was totally different to ours. Our method of de-colonization really reflected the pragmatic, almost accidental, way we acquired the empire. We divested ourselves of it in much the same way.

How much of British policy, as we come down to the final act in southern Africa, is accounted for by the sheer momentum of the 'de-colonizing' process?

The great watershed of course was India. We had acquired a great deal of the rest of the empire because of India, and the need to protect communications with India. Once the sub-continent had gone, although I don't think people necessarily thought in these terms at the time, it was inevitable that the rest would go; and the pattern on which the sub-continent had become independent would be followed in the rest of the empire.

But the British empire was an empire of settlement as well as of subjugation. Rhodesia was a part of the empire of settlement and had been accorded, in practice, virtually dominion status.

That is why we had such terrible problems with Rhodesia (and, to a lesser extent, Kenya). We were fortunate that in areas of the world which we settled, like Canada, Australia and New Zealand, there were no powerful indigenous communities. It was because of the *way* in which we had originally colonized that we had such appalling problems where we *did* have settled British communities living among large indigenous populations. The French method made that a bit easier. Even in Algeria, although the French fought the most bloody civil war there, they had 'frenchified' the north African Algerians to a far greater extent than we had 'anglicized' the black Rhodesians or South Africans.

But our insistence upon 'one man, one vote' was actively subversive of the

British national interest in a way that the French encouragement of the elites in Africa was not, and was more in tune with the African tribal structures, which were hierarchical.

I think that is quite true. Of course, 'one man, one vote' was a fairly late development in our de-colonization process. It all happened so quickly. There was not very much 'one man, one vote' going on in most of the empire – except for the settled parts, like Australia and New Zealand – right up to the 1950s. We very hurriedly had to put these structures in place when we realized that we were actually going to be 'off' within a few years.

At different times, and in different places, the British had been both Athenians and Romans under the Pax Britannica. The overseas empire was one of settlement as well as subjectdom. It was the difference between colonialism and imperialism. With Britain's great leap forward in Africa and the expansion of settlement led by Cecil Rhodes, colonialism took over where the advance of imperialism had halted, at the Cape. By the turn of the century colonialism had become the tail that wagged the Whitehall dog. It became policy to devolve power to the colonial territories. But into *whose* hands was not explicitly stated. At this point the ambiguities which arose became most acute concerning Rhodesia, which was almost wholly, but never quite, a self-governing dominion. Thereafter it seemed impossible to clear the British mind. **Sir Michael Palliser** again:

This was never understood by the world outside, but Rhodesia was not a colony in the standard sense. We had in fact given a measure of independence to the Rhodesian whites, years before, which could not be clawed back. This was, I suppose, the reason – going right back to the original declaration of independence[38] – why we did not send in troops. I mean, that we did not actually *have* a colonial presence in Rhodesia. The Rhodesian whites ran themselves. So, here was a situation for which the world saw us as responsible, and for which we saw ourselves as responsible, but which was extremely difficult to handle because we did not have the instruments accompanying that responsibility. We did have them, for example, in countries like Cyprus or Kenya.

To hold the scales impartially, in terms of history, would you agree that there was a certain logic to Mr Smith's illegal declaration of independence,

38 Ian Smith's illegal declaration – UDI – in 1965.

going back to the 1920s, and the Devonshire Agreement?[39] *The British said that former colonial territories were to become self-governing. We did not exactly say into* whose *hands power was to be delivered.*

I think there was complete logic and, of course, at the time when we allowed Rhodesia to go its own way,[40] no one was thinking in terms of black majority rule. It just wasn't conceivable at that time. So I do think, from the point of view of the Rhodesian whites, there was a logic to it. Of course, they did not carry the logic to its *logical* conclusion which, whatever you feel about apartheid, the South African whites *have* done. They simply say, 'This is *our* system, *we* are going to run this country, we're not going to allow 'one man one vote' and that's *that.*' The Rhodesian whites were mixed up about it. That is one of the reasons why the South African whites, on the whole, rather despise them. They saw them as people who had not got the courage of their convictions.

The British, it is said, would sooner collide in the middle of the road than anywhere else. In the end, Ian Smith too had been compelled to follow this tradition of compromise when, under duress, he accepted the *principle* of majority rule. White Rhodesian opinion had advanced beyond Harold Macmillan's experience when, after his 'wind of change' speech in Cape Town in 1960, and during his subsequent visit to Salisbury, he happened upon baboons 'making a nuisance of themselves' in the grounds of his hotel, one of them wearing a placard around its neck with the legend, 'one man, one vote'.[41] 'One man, one vote' had paved the way for the British withdrawal from India, where parliamentary democracy on the model of Westminster had proved a successful transplant. In 1979, as the Foreign Secretary was about to set the same de-colonizing 'machinery' first used in India in motion once more for Rhodesia, **Lord Carrington** had had to take a view of 'one man, one vote' as an African experience.

That has been the problem that we have always had, in de-colonization, hasn't it? Over the years, we have given constitutions around the world, based upon our Westminster constitution, which have not lasted. In retrospect, I think they do not necessarily suit everybody.

39 In 1923 the Duke of Devonshire, Colonial Secretary of the day in Bonar Law's government, issued a declaration that in any conflict of interest the British government would regard that of the African as 'paramount'.

40 In 1923.

41 Recounted by Sir Harold Evans, Macmillan's Press Secretary, in his *Downing Street Diary – the Macmillan Years* (London, Hodder and Stoughton, 1981), p. 101.

You may not think it suits *us* very well sometimes, when you look at what goes on in Parliament! But, on the whole, we've made it work. It's a good deal more difficult for some African states to make it work, because Africa is still, basically, a tribal system that operates on consensus. The Africans think that the confrontational aspects of the Westminster system are very curious, and they don't understand it at all. They think that the Opposition, decrying everything a government does, even though *they* did the same thing themselves when they were in office, and probably will do so again when they're in government next time, is a funny way to run the business. Africans try and do it on the basis of consensus. We may not think that 'consensus' leads to very democratic government in the sense that it very often leads to a one-party state – and, in the case of a many African countries, to a leader who remains there for ever because it's impossible to shift him!

Therefore, how far would you put yourself in sympathy with the views of somebody like Lord Caradon,[42] *who was in Papua New Guinea, I remember – one of the most remote of colonial situations – as the representative of the United Nations Trusteeship Council? He said, at Lae in New Guinea, for the benefit of the very few white Australians there, but speaking to the large crowd assembled of native New Guineans, 'Democracy is the ability of this man here to say, I want that man over there to represent me.' Is that how you saw the issue of 'one man, one vote'?*

That is how I would like to see it. I don't think I ever thought it was going to lead to the *ideal.* After all, one was not *blind.* One could see what had happened in other African countries. But it did not seem to me that there was any other way in which you could give independence to a country, unless you actually gave those people the opportunity to vote, and indeed, in Rhodesia, they *did* have the opportunity to vote, and they've *still* got the opportunity to vote. So, I think in that sense it *did* work, yes.

If you thought there was no other way, were there not other models? For your part, had you reflected on the way the French had behaved in black Africa after the colonial period? They maintained a hierarchical system, the 'district commissioner' system. They made no concessions to 'one man, one vote'. Power changed hands, yes, but not to majority rule.

But you are not talking about a situation in which you were giving a country independence *from scratch.* You are talking of a situation in which there had been a unilateral declaration of independence, an

42 Then Sir Hugh Foot, Ambassador to the United Nations and UK representative on the Trusteeship Council 1961–2.

illegal government, and a civil war which had lasted over some thirteen or fourteen years. You were not talking about sitting down and deciding how it would be *best* to do it. You were faced with the reality. The reality was that the only way in which you could get a settlement was, first of all, that there should be 'one man, one vote', because that was something which we were pledged to do. Secondly, there was no way in which you could have got the white Rhodesian to accept any settlement which did not involve some kind of Westminster-type constitution like that which was operating before. Those were the *realities* you had to deal with. It's no good saying what would have been ideal. What you were faced with is what was *possible.*

By 1979, how did you measure the cumulative effect on politics in Britain, and for the conduct of our foreign policy, of the need to defend and debate 'Rhodesia'?

Internally, it was becoming more and more difficult to do that, of course. I had some personal experience. I was Leader of the Opposition in the Lords under two Labour governments, and to get the House of Lords to agree every year to the continuation of sanctions was, to say the least, rather difficult. That was obviously going to be increasingly difficult, under a Conservative government, after the election of Bishop Muzorewa in Rhodesia. It was certainly one of the internal factors that made it urgently necessary to try and get a settlement.

We no longer just wanted a settlement, we needed *a settlement?*

We needed a settlement. The question was whether it was possible to get one.

But, as you set out to try and get a settlement, what was your underlying objective? Was it to secure a moderate pro-Western government or was it to settle *it?*

Oh, not settle it *at any price*, but on the basis of what we had always said – the majority rule to which we were pledged. Obviously, we *hoped* that it was going to be a pro-Western type of government and maybe you hoped, one way or the other, who would compose it. But, if you accept that majority rule is what you are aiming for, you are not in much of a position to dictate what happens after it.

Lord Carrington therefore brought to his determination to settle the Rhodesia question the art of the possible, but no over-arching concept.

The government itself was at first divided. Mrs Thatcher had sent out Lord Boyd,[43] a former Colonial Secretary, to observe the elections in 1979 which had produced Bishop Muzorewa as Prime Minister of a predominantly black administration. Boyd had reported that those elections were 'free and fair'. Then, the Prime Minister, in Canberra on her way home from an economic summit in Japan in July 1979, had echoed there the manifesto commitment on Rhodesia on which the Conservatives had been elected at the British general election that May.[44] In saying that Britain would find it difficult to re-impose sanctions against Rhodesia, but that 'recognition might take a little longer', Mrs Thatcher had appeared to confirm the intention of moving to recognize Bishop Muzorewa's government and Ian Smith's internal settlement. Her remarks produced an immediate outcry, coming as they did less than a month before the Commonwealth heads of government were due to meet in August, in Lusaka, where Rhodesia would be top of the agenda.

Mrs Thatcher was headed for a major confrontation. Given the constraints of the governing 'realities' we have seen listed by Lord Carrington, how did **Julian Amery** think that the Conservative election pledge was now to be understood?

> *I* understood it, and indeed Mrs Thatcher in her speech in Australia shortly before the Lusaka conference appeared to make it plain, that on the strength of Lord Boyd's recommendation we would recommend to Parliament that we lift the sanctions and recognize Rhodesia as a member of the Commonwealth. To be a member of the Commonwealth, of course, we would have had to get the acceptance of the others.
>
> *So, we must look for reasons why – in this short space between the Prime Minister's statement in Canberra, which appeared to confirm her long-term intentions of lifting sanctions and moving to recognize the Bishop – the British government, with its mandate to do that, now changes its mind?*
>
> Many influences were at work. There was the Foreign Office. I remember, because I had been in the Office, between 1972 and 1974. We'd had many discussions on the Rhodesian problem, and Lord

43 Formerly Alan Lennox-Boyd, Secretary of State for the Colonies 1954–9. Set up the Central African Federation in September 1953.

44 This said '. . . if the six principles which all British governments have supported for the last fifteen years are fully satisfied following the recent election, the next government will have the duty to return Rhodesia to a state of legality, move to lift sanctions, and do its utmost to see that the new independent state gains international recognition.'

Home[45] had moved very far towards recognition, supporting the formation of a multi-racial government, which actually took place after we'd left office. But, there was very great resistance on the part of officials: partly, because they feared the repercussions on African opinion in the rest of the continent; partly because they feared for our economic position in those countries, although the only important stake was the oil in Nigeria, which *they* cancelled anyway, so it wasn't even a bargaining weapon for *them*. Then, there was the influence of the churches, particularly the Nonconformist in Scotland, which had a long association with Africa, the 'Exeter Hall connection',[46] if you like, which goes back to the last century.

Dr Livingstone?

Yes. There was the influence of Mr Cyrus Vance,[47] who would have been very much against recognition, but who was doomed that year to leave office and make way for people with a very different outlook. Then there was Lord Carrington. I have a great affection and admiration for Lord Carrington. I think he is a marvellous negotiator who did make a great ambassador, when he was High Commissioner in Australia,[48] and I think diplomacy is his art. But I think he mistook diplomacy for foreign policy. *Diplomacy* is the practice of negotiating and seeking agreement. *Foreign policy* is to have a concept of where your interests lie, *then* get your diplomats to pursue them. I think the idea of pulling off a deal which would please everybody was immensely attractive to him. Although I think the consequences have been tragic, at the time of Lancaster House, it was hailed as a triumph. Many who had doubts about it were so impressed by the consensus that emerged that even *they* hailed it as a success. Mrs Thatcher herself had little choice but to do the same.

None the less, the battle for the Prime Minister's mind in those few short weeks between Canberra and the Lusaka conference is an important one.

Oh very. But she was not established. She had just got into power. Half the Cabinet were less than wholeheartedly supporting her. She was, relatively, still a novice in foreign policy. And to go against her Foreign Secretary, and against the Foreign Office, and against many in the Cabinet, would have been a very difficult operation. I can never

45 Foreign Secretary in Edward Heath's government 1970–4.

46 Exeter Hall, in the Strand, was let for large religious and especially missionary assemblies in the nineteenth century. In 1880 it was purchased for the YMCA.

47 US Secretary of State in President Carter's administration, 1977–80.

48 From November 1956 to October 1959.

believe that she was enthusiastic about what she did, but I think she reckoned she had to bite on the bullet, and that it was not *all-important.*

The principle of black majority rule had been established in Rhodesia with Bishop Abel Muzorewa's election. The issue then became the extent to which it was genuine majority rule. The Bishop might have become Rhodesia's first black Prime Minister, but his victory did not meet the objectives of the leaders of the front-line states, in particular Presidents Kaunda of Zambia and Samora Machel of Mozambique, whose countries were hosts to the fighting forces of the Patriotic Front. If the Bishop's voice was the voice of Jacob, the hand, to them, was the hand of Esau! That is, the continued influence of Ian Smith in Muzorewa's government was anathema.

The most compelling of Lord Carrington's 'realities' was that Bishop Muzorewa's election pledge to end the war could not be sustained. Indeed, the war was intensifying. The Bishop's ability to fulfil his pledge depended, to some extent at least, on perceptions of Muzorewa as a nationalist leader with wide popular support. Historians will clearly be interested in why it was that **Bishop Abel Muzorewa** did so well in the election of April 1979 in Rhodesia, Ian Smith's 'internal settlement', and so badly in the 'independence' election which followed it in May 1980 and which brought Robert Mugabe to power.

I am sure they will be *very* interested. I would hope that among the people who came and observed that last election, there will be some courageous souls who will say what a pathetic situation it was. Because there were cadres, guerrillas or 'freedom-fighters' almost everywhere in the country. While everybody was asleep, the people were being collected like a bunch of sheep and told, 'You shall vote Mugabe or, after the election, you are dead.' I hope that somebody is going to say that is what happened. As far as I am concerned it *is* one of the explanations. There are other speculations, which I will not go into, because I don't have evidence. However, the fact is, some people think the election was rigged. I am a Christian and I do not wish to pass judgement on things for which I do not have evidence. But, as to the first, I *do* have evidence for that.

But, unable to end the war, do you agree that belief in your government, as a government of national unity, was further eroded when the Reverend Ndabaningi Sithole[49] *decided to boycott the new parliament and claimed your April 1979 election was rigged?*

49 A former leader of ZANU (Zimbabwe African National Union), replaced as leader by Robert Mugabe in 1974.

Well, the Reverend Ndabaningi Sithole's history shows that he never accepted anyone, from *any* of the political parties, as a leader. It either had to be him or no one. It was face-saving on his part. How, otherwise, was he to explain to the people – he who had been a politician long before I had come on the scene – why he had failed in the election? So, we do not take that very seriously. I agree that we were embarrassed, because we were supposed to be a government of national unity.

There is a spectacular difference between the two Rhodesian elections of April 1979 and that won by Mr Mugabe in March 1980. In Mashonaland West, for example, you got 83 per cent of the votes in 1979, and won all six seats, and less than a year later you had 10 per cent of the vote and won only one seat. What is your explanation for that?

What I have just said.

That intimidation decided the outcome?

That is right.

Clearly, your ability to fulfil your election pledge to end the war depended on the response to the amnesty you offered to the forces of the Patriotic Front, led from Zambia by Joshua Nkomo and from Mozambique by Robert Mugabe. That response must have rested, to some extent, on whether they saw you as a genuine nationalist leader. Why do you believe there was a poor response to that offer of amnesty?

Because, in the first place, the people whom we called the leaders of the 'front-line states', while helping us, were at the same time 'king-makers'. They had certain persons tailored to rule Zimbabwe, and I am sure that they were disappointed when I became Prime Minister. So, along with the local Rhodesian African leaders, I think they made up their mind that they were going to fight very hard to defeat that. It became a question, not of *principles*, such as 'majority rule', for which we had been fighting, but a question of who should be the leader. Therefore, they intensified the war. I was not expecting that. I had hoped that people would be united, especially as the one thing for which we had been struggling all these years, majority rule, had been achieved. If I had made up my mind that I was *not* going to give up, that I would go on fighting just to shed blood, I think we could have gone on for some time and, I'm sure, finally won. But, I thought, if it would save bloodshed I would rather we did not continue to be in that situation.

How should we judge this question of whether you were a leader in name only, or whether this was a genuine prospect of black majority rule?

As far as I am concerned, and I think to anyone who is well versed in this situation, it was genuine. First of all, the principle of majority rule *had* been achieved. We were able to enfranchise persons of this country eighteen years of age and above. This meant that we now had the power to do whatever we wanted to do.

I admit that, in the first stage of our arrangement, we had too many whites – about eight too many – however, I felt that it was good that we should try to keep the confidence of the whites. But, like any country, we were then going to improve upon that situation, changing the constitution as we go. Mr Mugabe has changed the constitution – all he wants – since Lancaster House. *We* were going to do the same. There was nothing that would stop us from doing that, because we had the majority in parliament.

None the less, the international attack upon you, particularly from the Patriotic Front and the front-line states, was that you were a pawn and a puppet of white Rhodesia.

If you ask them 'What do you mean?' all they will say is, 'Because you gave the whites too many seats,' and I have given you my reason for that. Temporarily, we had to do that. But we knew that, as we went on, the constitution would be perfected.

Would you agree that the hotting up of the war by the Patriotic Front made it impossible for you to carry out the economic and social reforms that you had in mind, and that you were being driven more and more, for economic and military support, into the arms of South Africa?

We had some problem in doing the reforms we wanted because of the intensification of the war, but we did quite a lot. For example, one of the thorns of this country – one of the real spears in the flesh – was the whole question of its discriminatory legislation. We scrapped that within a few months. So we *did* do some very important reform. We changed a whole list of things within six months during my government. We improved the teachers' salaries; we set up development in the rural areas; we set up a system whereby the poor Africans could set up a business and get loans and return the money gradually. We were not doing that badly considering our short time. In fact, if you listen to the people who want to be honest, and who are not *afraid*, they will tell you that we did a lot more in six months than the Mugabe government has done in twelve or eighteen months!

You think that you're entitled to a different verdict from history?

I believe that when the country becomes sober, and the historians also become fair-minded, they would put me down in history as the George

Washington of Zimbabwe. I believe that is exactly the role I played for this country.

Then after Lord Boyd's assessment that your own election in April 1979 had been both 'free and fair', and then Mrs Thatcher's new Conservative government taking office just a few weeks later, what were your expectations?

My hope and expectation was that because our election had been declared 'free and fair', and because we had organized it on the basis of majority rule, they were going to recognize it. They have recognized people who have come out of the bush with guns, and who stage coups – within twenty-four hours! Why would they not recognize a government that had been freely elected, with a clear majority? We expected them to do so. We were very disappointed – in fact very angry – when they did not.

Before the Bishop was forced to step aside he had shown no strong indications of greatness. But then neither, in earlier life, had George Washington. However, as Bishop Muzorewa would no doubt concede, Washington was in the end successful. Lord Carrington could not bring himself to counsel recognition of the Bishop. All accounts agree that Mrs Thatcher was irritated by the Foreign Office's pessimism. Most of those close to the Prime Minister favoured cutting the Gordian knot and recognizing the internal settlement. The themes of racial equality were not uppermost among the Prime Minister's preoccupations. She was impatient of autocratic African governments that had made a mess of their economies, and of Third World majorities in the Commonwealth and the United Nations laying down the law to her. How is one to see her at this time? If for Harold Wilson as Prime Minister, fifteen years earlier, it had been a question of 'having to win' in Rhodesia against Ian Smith, like Kennedy having to win over Cuba, can it be said with precision how Rhodesia presented itself to Mrs Thatcher? Her Parliamentary Private Secretary at the time was **Ian Gow**, an informed confidant and, where Mrs Thatcher was concerned, a keeper of the true flame.

Certainly the Prime Minister's instincts were always against sanctions. Initially, she wanted to recognize the Muzorewa government. That, I think, was her hope. One has to remember that, in the period before 1979, although Rhodesia was an important issue, it was not one which attracted a great amount of Mrs Thatcher's time. She was enormously concerned with the economic priorities at home; with policies which would restore the economy and with introducing changes in the trade union law. It was only after she became Prime Minister that it was necessary for her to address herself, in much greater detail, to the

Rhodesian problem. I believe that there was a change in her judgement. I think her initial view, in May 1979, and during the election campaign – and indeed, in the months before that – was to recognize the Muzorewa government. She hoped that that would have brought an end to, or a substantial reduction in, terrorism; and that she would have been able to *do* that, and then achieve international recognition.

Margaret Thatcher had been taken aback, during her visit to Canberra on 1 July 1979, by the trenchancy with which the Australian Prime Minister, Malcolm Fraser, had maintained that Australia would line up with the front-line states in the forthcoming Commonwealth heads of government meeting in Lusaka and against any concessions to Muzorewa and Smith. On her return to London, she was further persuaded that recognition of the Bishop would not lead to an end of Rhodesia's civil struggle, but probably to its getting worse, and that the international recognition she had specifically included in the Conservative manifesto would not be forthcoming.

No sharp downpour of congratulations greeted the Foreign Office advice to the Prime Minister that what she had wanted to do would achieve neither objective. The Foreign Office, as **Ian Gow** knew, was *not* Mrs Thatcher's favourite department.

It is true to say that the Prime Minister did *not* believe, in May 1979, in the infallibility of the Foreign Office! I think it would be true to say that Lord Carrington had a significant influence on the Prime Minister. She liked Lord Carrington, and respected him greatly, not lease because he had had a very considerable experience of overseas and Commonwealth affairs. He had been our High Commissioner in Canberra and Secretary for Defence in Mr Heath's government. She had chosen him as her Foreign Secretary rather than Mr Pym, who had been Shadow Foreign Secretary until the general election. Certainly, in the very clear way in which he always used to describe the obstacles that lay in her path, the advantages of one course and the disadvantages of another, Lord Carrington had strong sway with the Prime Minister. You have also got to remember that although Mrs Thatcher had made journeys overseas as Leader of the Opposition, it was presumed to be the area of policy with which she was least familiar.

Should we think that Lord Carrington was successful in appealing to the sense of adventure in the Prime Minister? That what he finally proposed – what caught her attention and won her support in the end – was his appeal to her that Britain had to take a strong, bold, if risky, initiative? In other words, the traditional appeals, the reality that 'the Commonwealth would not like it', or that 'the United Nations would make great difficulties', were not deeply attractive to Mrs Thatcher, who was a bit jaundiced about both?

You are perfectly correct. The view of the United Nations was *not* something which weighed very heavily with Mrs Thatcher. As more recent events about sanctions have shown,[50] the Prime Minister will not be deflected from a course which she thinks is right simply because other countries disagree with that course. Although the policy we followed *was* bold and imaginative and had a certain risk, it became clear that the original strategy of recognition of the Muzorewa government would have carried a greater risk.

Before making such decisions, all Prime Ministers have to make their own judgement about the weight and character of those involved.

There is the story of Churchill, at the time when he was predisposing what proved to be the post-war politics of Greece, asking General Scobie[51] *in Athens*[52] *to size up Archbishop Damaskinos.*[53] *Churchill is reported to have said, 'Are we dealing with a man of God, on his knees before the Almighty in daily supplication, or a scheming priest with a political ambition?' to which, when Scobie answered, 'I very much regret to say, Prime Minister, I believe it is more the latter,' Churchill replied,* 'Then he's our man!' *Let us apply that to the judgement that had to be made of Bishop Muzorewa. What impression had Bishop Muzorewa made on Mrs Thatcher?*

I like your quotation very much. One of the sadnesses about that period in 1978 and 1979 was that the Bishop, who I'm sure was a man of God, was without any political skills at all. If there *had* been, at the head of the then 'internal' Rhodesian government, a man of outstanding political skill and quality, a leader who commanded very considerable support within Rhodesia, then it might have been a different story. But, amongst the tragedies of Rhodesia was the fact that the Bishop was really not a politician at all.

So, after Mrs Thatcher had met the Bishop she believed him unsuited to the exactions of modern politics, let alone capable of ending a war. This became one of the major considerations in the course of the

50 A reference to Mrs Thatcher's continued opposition to sanctions against South Africa.

51 General Sir Ronald Scobie, Commander of the British forces in Greece 1944–6.

52 During Churchill's visit in December 1944.

53 The Archbishop of Athens whom Churchill wished to appoint Regent.

intensive briefings by the Foreign Office officials, and discussions with **Lord Carrington**, during which the Prime Minister was talked round, it seems, by sheer devastation of argument.

I think the Prime Minister took all the arguments. We discussed this over a long period of time and she understood as well as I did all the arguments for and against. The Conservative Party, frankly, was in a difficult position: because Lord Boyd, who after all is one of the most respected of Conservatives, was asked to go out and find out whether the election of Bishop Muzorewa was fair, and he came back and said that, in his judgement, it *was* fair. That, of course, made it very difficult for the Conservative government not to accept the result. I think you could argue it both ways. I still believe that the consequences of accepting that election – and the Prime Minister agreed with me – were really such that no British government ought to do so before they had one more try at settling it on a basis in which *everybody* could be involved.

But is it right to suggest, or to conclude, that Mrs Thatcher instinctively favoured recognition whereas you did not?

You must remember that, in 1979, the Prime Minister had not had much experience of foreign affairs. I do not say that in any critical way. I think that, politically, she was in a very difficult position; for all these reasons, and the fact that Lord Boyd went out there. Therefore she was perfectly right, instinctively, to think that that was the right solution. But, when we started to talk about it, and to see what the consequences were for British foreign policy, for the British economy, for the future of the Commonwealth in so far as that matters – and I, personally, still think it *does* matter – for our position in the European Community and in the world generally, then I believed we ought to reflect whether we ought to accept this quite so quickly as we might have done, perhaps, had we not considered these other issues. I think she understood that, and was as convinced as I was by it.

Can you remember the moment of her convincing? She comes to power with a much more combative attitude than her predecessors about the 'wind of change', more hotly disputing any suggestion that the British were tired or had lost their will. Margaret Thatcher wanted to be much tougher about such things. 'One man one vote' had led more often than not to black autocracies and what she saw as a lack of regard for human rights. What, in the end, convinced her?

Her intelligence, her intellect, convinced her that this would not be the right thing to do until you had had *one more try* to settle it. She was perfectly right. You know, having worked with the Prime Minister over a number of years, the one thing that stands out about her is this. If you make a case to her, which to her seems to 'stand up', and is logical, she listens to it and makes up her own mind about whether it is right or wrong. I have not found, as some people have said, that she is 'intransigent' and all the rest of it. It always seemed to me that, if you argued a case with her which made some sense and convinced her, there was no problem.

Whereas Julian Amery felt that because the Prime Minister was 'not established' she therefore 'had to bite the bullet'[54] over Rhodesia, we have Lord Carrington's word for it that Mrs Thatcher became intellectually convinced and, after being thoroughly marinated in all the arguments, persuaded, that the Foreign Secretary should embark on the great effort to which his talents now consigned him – bringing to an agreed end the long, unhappy story of illegally independent Rhodesia.

The nature of the final outcome remained a leap in the dark. The ultimate victor, Robert Mugabe, compared with other nationalist leaders, like Joshua Nkomo, at this stage was little known. Mugabe had been educated by the Jesuits who, at their mission near Salisbury, had preached 'equality'. Later he had embraced Marxism, after which, Mr Mugabe had let many cats out of his bag. He let it be known that he based his political actions on those of a terrible disturber, Lenin. As **Robert Mugabe**'s hour was approaching, following his years of detention by Ian Smith, then exile in Mozambique, how successful had he been in widening the aims of his ZANU party to include both talk and action for a new society, based on the teachings of Marx and Lenin?

Any liberation struggle, and I would like to believe any war at all, especially a 'just war', must have a political direction. In our own case the political direction had to have within it an inner *ideological* direction. This is why we always said that 'politics direct the gun.' The trajectory of our guns, we said, was *political.* We did not shoot for the sake of shooting; we shot because we had political objectives that stood to be achieved. Therefore we had to create quite a high level of political and ideological consciousness.

The leadership itself had to be very clear what the liberation struggle was about because, if the leadership was not clear, it could not expect the ordinary people to be clear. So, the starting point was to make the fighters more ideologically conscious. You always had a political

54 See p. 28.

commissar. What had the political commissar to do, by way of his own function? He had to be *political* and *ideological.* He had to motivate the fighters. He had to inspire them, and all the time tell the story that our fight was just; that we were there to overhaul the system as it stood, and create a more just system based on majority rule. *Democracy* was therefore to be the basis of our own political system.

Joaquim Chissano, the President of Mozambique, when he was Foreign Minister, is on the record at another time – when he was seeking to reassure people who were alarmed at the prospect of your heading a government in Rhodesia – that you were not *a Marxist. He said 'He is not a Marxist as we are Marxists here, in Mozambique, with FRELIMO.'*[55] *How are we to understand this difference?*

I don't know what difference they saw. I *suppose* the difference was that perhaps themselves, having been more associated with the Soviet Union, the GDR, Cuba and the rest, had a wider spectrum of ideological and political associates. They perhaps felt, at the time, that their own understanding of Marxism–Leninism was higher than our own, which was quite false.

I still remember the first time I met the late President Samora Machel[56] and we were talking about revolution. He actually posed the question to me, 'What is a revolution?' I would have brushed his question aside as an insult in other circumstances, but I chose to reply and tell him what I conceived to be a revolution. I suppose they wanted to know whether I *understood* what I said. They did not know me at all. In my own study of politics I had done quite a lot of reading about Marxism–Leninism. When I went 'outside'[57] to try and lead ZANU, that became an environment in which I felt – with the background our cadres then had of being associated with the Chinese, and the Mao Tse Tung philosophy, and his version of Marxism–Leninism – that I could develop my *own* thinking in a practical way.

How should we summarize this? Did you see Marxism–Leninism as a useful tool, or as a total explanation?

Both. I saw it as an explanation, and as a tool. But also as a most desirable state of things at the end of the day in our socio-economic

55 The Front for the Liberation of Mozambique, which became active in 1962 and launched its 'armed struggle' against Portuguese rule, culminating in the achievement of independence in 1975.

56 Chissano succeeded Machel as President of Mozambique following the latter's death in an air crash in 1986 near the Mozambique border with South Africa.

57 I.e. to Mozambique.

> system. Not that I believed that *everything* that Marx said would apply; nor did I believe that all that Lenin did, by way of applying Marxism in the Soviet Union, would work here. We always said, in the final analysis, that our Marxism–Leninism would have to adapt itself to our own situation, and take into account our own history, and our own tradition – history meaning, of course, also the history of colonialism and its effect upon our society and upon our people. Whatever we did, therefore, would have to take these objective factors into account.

Because Mr Mugabe's beliefs and actions were rooted in the class struggle, compromise seemed a poor prospect. Yet, with the rich glint of hindsight, it would become clear that in the autumn of 1979 *all* parties to the Rhodesia dispute needed a settlement. All, that is, except Mr Mugabe, who thought he was bound to win in the end anyway. But a rare coincidence of opportunities was forming which at the time seemed improbable. Mrs Thatcher had changed her mind, but was not yet wholly convinced. That had to wait for what happened in Lusaka, where the peacocks screech on the lawns outside President Kaunda's tiny study and where the basis was laid for a stunning diplomatic achievement.

2

'Dearest Margaret'

Looking back, the future of Britain's last colony in Africa was settled at Lusaka at the meeting of all the heads of Commonwealth governments in August 1979. The understanding arrived at there proved strong enough to weather all the storms that followed. But, as British ministers set out for this crucial conference, the omens could hardly have looked less promising. The outlook called to mind a despatch to the Foreign Office by a British ambassador in another time, and from another place, which said, 'It is impossible to exaggerate the gravity of the present situation, but *I will do my best*'! Mrs Thatcher's most recent public utterance on Rhodesia had been in July, the month before Lusaka, in Canberra. There she had found herself at odds with the Australian Prime Minister, Malcolm Fraser, in suggesting that Britain might proceed to recognize the outcome of Ian Smith's internal settlement with the Rhodesian African leaders. But, after thrashing out all the arguments with Lord Carrington and the Foreign Office, on her return from Australia, the Prime Minister now accepted that an effort must be made to get a wider settlement. The African leaders, for their part, were unaware of Mrs Thatcher's change of direction, which was revealed, and indeed only fully completed, in Lusaka. As the leaders of all the Commonwealth governments flew to Zambia, destiny advanced and the hour was heavy with events and portents. The chairman of the Lusaka conference was a son of the Church, and a recognized champion of African nationalism since the 1950s, the President of Zambia, **Kenneth Kaunda**.

> We were quite clear in our minds that the man behind the problem was Ian Douglas-Smith. Having gone through all that we did with him at the helm there was no way we could trust him. All power was in his hands. Bishop Muzorewa was a mere accomplice. The *real* power was with Ian Smith and, therefore, in Pretoria. At any time Ian

Douglas-Smith could manipulate the dull Bishop to his advantage. We would not accept that. Defence and security matters were all controlled by Ian Douglas-Smith. The Bishop was a mere puppet of the white racist regime, and all the people in power were really Ian Douglas-Smith impostors. It was because of the *freedom-fighter* that Smith changed from declaring that there would be no black government in Rhodesia 'in a thousand years'. And so, the *real* power to effect the change, which successive British governments had failed to do, was with the freedom-fighter.

But do you agree that the Patriotic Front, which had failed to disrupt or prevent Muzorewa's election, was at this time, immediately before the Lusaka conference, well short of its most optimistic objectives?

No. I would say the very fact that Ian Douglas-Smith had taken that step – to put a 'puppet' in his own place – was an indication that he had begun to feel the pressure of the freedom-fighter. From that point onwards it was only a matter of time.

Over the years you had many opportunities to make a judgement of Mr Smith. In coming out against his internal settlement, how important was your experience at the time of the showdown with him, and Present Vorster of South Africa, and Mr Nkomo, at Victoria Falls, in 1975[1] *– your last big effort to induce Ian Smith to accept black government?*

Perhaps we should go back, first, to the time when we were ending the Rhodesian Federation.[2] I remember asking that great Englishman, Sir Evelyn Hone,[3] at the end of the conference with the late 'Rab' Butler[4] in the chair, 'Please let me meet the Rhodesian Prime Minister because, as we become independent, in the future Zambia, these people are going to be under great pressure. Let me offer them our good offices.' The good man did that for me. I met the Rhodesian Prime Minister, the late Winston Field.[5] He came with someone else I had never seen before. It was Ian Douglas-Smith. We sat down together. I said to Winston Field, 'Look, Mr Prime Minister, I'm

1 A conference held in a railway carriage on the Victoria Falls Bridge, opened for the occasion by the Zambians. This was an effort by Kaunda and Vorster to promote the latter's concept of 'détente'.

2 The dissolution conference winding up the Central African Federation was held at the Victoria Falls on 28 June–4 July 1963 (see notes 21 and 43 to chapter 1).

3 Governor of Northern Rhodesia 1959–64.

4 Lord Butler, First Secretary of State and Deputy Prime Minister at this time and the minister in charge of the Central African Office.

5 Prime Minister of Southern Rhodesia 1962–4 and President of the Rhodesia Front Party 1962–5. In 1964 he stepped down to be succeeded by Ian Smith.

quite clear in my mind that you – let me call you *white nationalists* – will soon be under pressure. Your fellow *black nationalists* will come up in arms. I would like to offer you our good offices. If you feel that we might be of use, playing the role of a bridge between the two nationalisms, please don't hesitate to approach us.' Winston Field looked at me, and he said, 'Mr Kaunda, if we did not know that you were sincere in what you are saying we would tell you to mind your own business!' I said, 'Very well. I *will* mind my own business.' That was in 1963. In 1965, UDI came. I kept my peace. I kept it until, one day, Ian Douglas-Smith found himself landing at our airstrip here, in Zambian Air Force helicopters. We met here for a number of hours. He asked us what we might do to reconcile the various groups within Rhodesia. I told him there was only one answer. Majority rule. Without that, nothing else could happen. This led to the meeting at the bridge[6] you talked about. All this was after we recognized that, while the British government was the colonial power *de jure, de facto* it was the racist regime of South Africa which really controlled the situation. It is a long story, but *that* is why I began sending my envoys to Vorster in South Africa, and why John Vorster sent his envoys here, until we agreed on what we believed would lead to majority rule in a constitutional arrangement. We put down some conditions. Vorster responded. Part of the deal was that the nationalist leaders, Robert Mugabe, Joshua Nkomo, and all the others, were released. *Then*, we went to the bridge, with Ian Douglas-Smith supported by John Vorster, and the nationalists supported by Zambia, and the other front-line states. We thought we would reach an agreement. After four days we did not. The meeting ended in turmoil. There was no way in which we could trust Ian Douglas-Smith with anything.

I am not quite sure why you think that Smith deceived you at the time of these talks with Vorster?

He deceived us because he had agreed with us, through Vorster – and we had pursued it from the beginning – that they would be moving step by step towards the ideal. Majority rule. It was not to be, because Ian Douglas-Smith withdrew his support.

Relations between Ian Smith and the South Africans were never quite the same after this particular meeting. It marked a point of departure. John Vorster considered that Ian Smith had reversed South Africa's previous understanding of Rhodesia's intentions. President Kaunda, for

6 I.e. the Victoria Falls meeting, August 1975.

his part, had been the key to Vorster's attempted 'détente' with the black states and had been dangerously exposed by its failure.

This is one episode, among many, which serves to illustrate the very great degree of mistrust that surrounded Ian Smith outside Rhodesia and the passionate scepticism which greeted his all the more extraordinary achievement of the internal settlement. Black government had clearly come to stay in Rhodesia with Bishop Muzorewa's election, in April 1979, and there could be no turning back. But, as Mrs Thatcher and Lord Carrington flew out to Lusaka in August – with all to play for – the chairman of the Commonwealth conference, **Kenneth Kaunda**, confesses to no little apprehension about Mrs Thatcher's intentions.

> She was a political leader and she had a programme drawn up by her party. The Tories were quite clear on this issue at their Party Conference, the previous year. We could only go by what the Tory Party had said they were going to do. The right wing, obviously, was very strong; and that, after all, is how Margaret Thatcher came to power. In addition, when she went to Australia, she made that terrifying statement. We were pinning all our hopes on Lusaka and we were frightened that 'the Iron Lady' would wish to implement her party's policies on this issue.
>
> We knew, first of all, that she knew nothing about Africa. Secondly, she would have to go by what her advisers said. The only person you could trust in that Tory collection of people was Peter Carrington, and we did not know how much influence he had on her. It was *that* influence versus the ultra-right-wingers in the Tory party. And, it was that inability, on her part, to state that she *was* going for majority rule in Rhodesia, which lent wings to our fears. We were quite clear in our minds that with the Commonwealth leaders coming to Lusaka, and getting the feel of things, *they* would be in favour of majority rule. The question was, how to convince the British government. When we met here, it became more and more clear that the issue was only whether the British Prime Minister would choose to stand all alone while the rest of the Commonwealth was saying, 'Go for it. Let's get majority rule in Zimbabwe!'

The African leaders, Kaunda included, were thus ignorant or unsure of Britain's real position. They were determined to press Mrs Thatcher into withholding recognition from Bishop Muzorewa. This was in fact what the Prime Minister had privately made up her mind to do; not, as was being demanded, by granting it to the Patriotic Front, but by convening a conference of all parties, including the leaders of the Patriotic Front, from outside Rhodesia. This moment of decision had come in London, during Mrs Thatcher's marination in all the arguments with the Foreign Office. Towards the end of one of these intensive briefings she had asked, finally, 'How did one de-colonize a colony which did *not* have a problem?'

Sensing a 'bringing-over' to an opinion not previously held, the Foreign Office had its historical answer ready – a constitutional conference. The art, as the British saw it, would be to induce the African leaders to *ask* for one.

While Rhodesia was generally regarded as the foreign policy issue on which the Conservative and Labour parties were furthest apart, Conservative governments were believed more able to 'deliver' on such issues. Expectations, generally, had been increased in consequence. At the same time, the Conservative Party's – and Mrs Thatcher's own – declarations had added the spice of a possible radical showdown with the rest of the Commonwealth. A barely muted hostility seemed almost the best the Prime Minister could hope for on arrival in Zambia, and she took dark glasses with her on the trip just in case, she said, 'someone throws acid or something at me'.[7]

Anticipation mounted, as under the gull's-eye of television, journalists of all the world ringed the Lusaka conference many ranks deep, in interrogative mood, and with the Prime Minister and **Lord Carrington** at bay.

It had been greatly trailed, as an event, by the media and, of course, at that time the Prime Minister had the reputation of being violently against any kind of settlement on the lines that we eventually agreed. Quite untrue: she was not; but *that* is the reputation she had. So, when the Prime Minister and I arrived in Lusaka, there was a general feeling that there was going to be an almighty bust-up, and that the Commonwealth would fall apart, and that the whole position would be really extremely unpleasant and difficult. It did not really turn out like that. It was much calmer than anybody had ever supposed it was going to be. I think that, certainly, it opened the Prime Minister's eyes to some of the African heads of state, and it opened the African Prime Ministers' eyes to her. As a result of that there was a good deal more understanding.

One of the misconceptions about what happened at Lusaka was that the British Government was *persuaded* to agree to Lancaster

7 Quoted in Patrick Cosgrave, *Thatcher – the First Term* (London, Bodley Head, 1979), p. 79.

House,[8] to *go along* with such a conference. That is absolutely untrue. *We went there with the proposal that this should happen*, and persuaded everybody to agree to it. It was not the other way round. We went to Lusaka to get agreement to a conference, at which we would have a final try at getting a solution to which everybody could subscribe.

In doing that, your ambition at Lusaka therefore was not to get the widest possible international agreement for the Smith–Muzorewa settlement?

No. It was to get an agreement on the Lancaster House conference.

Had you not *got that, what was your minimum position? What was the least you could emerge with from Lusaka?*

I don't think you could have had anything more 'minimal' than that. You could not have got *less* than that and made a solution practicable. Either you got that, or you had to go ahead and recognize the Muzorewa government.

As Lord Carrington and the Prime Minister were fastening their seat-belts for Lusaka, there was a frown from black Africa before which Britain was meant to tremble. Of all the African states, only one was in a position to threaten Britain directly with economic reprisals of a significant order. This was Nigeria, Britain's biggest trading partner in Africa and a major source of oil during those years of the 'energy crisis' induced by the oil cartel, OPEC. On the eve of the Lusaka conference, Nigeria nationalized all the oil production and marketing facilities of British Petroleum.

Nigeria's head of state at that time was General Olusegun Obasanjo. The General lives today on his farm outside Lagos. A prominent notice on the large iron-clad doors of its entrance gateway says 'No robbers, hawkers or media allowed'. It accords with the owner's forcible character. The General is a graduate of the Mons Officers Cadet School at Aldershot, and robust in word and action. The stone walls and floors of the farmhouse reverberate with a voice accustomed to command. **General Olusegun Obasanjo** believes Nigeria's act in expropriating British Petroleum played its part in compelling Britain to alter course away from the Conservative manifesto pledge on Rhodesia – even if it was an intervention that outraged Lord Carrington.

Lord Carrington went to our Foreign Minister,[9] not only losing his

8 The constitutional conference in London, which closely followed the Lusaka meeting of Commonwealth heads of government at which agreement to hold it was reached.

9 General Adefope.

cool but almost with his fist in his face, and saying, 'You will regret that action. It's nonsense!' So, they *were* surprised. I forget who it was in Britain who had referred to Nigeria as 'a toothless bulldog', which meant that we could bark but not bite. What happened, of course, is that things had been taken for granted in the past. Nothing *had* happened.

A bit of a risk to suggest to the military leader of Nigeria that he is 'a toothless bulldog'. Did you find that remark provocative?

It *was* provocative. But, I think the man who made that statement was probably justified. We had had many leaders in Nigeria before, and things did *not* happen. We had shouted before, but never gone beyond shouting.

Can we be sure of your position before Lusaka? What were the dominant themes in your decision not to back the Bishop's government in Rhodesia?

Just as we felt that any solution that excluded the British government was no solution, we felt that any solution that excluded the fighting forces outside Rhodesia was no solution. That is not to say that the forces *inside* Rhodesia could be ignored. We were not involved in personalities but in principles. We did not think the Bishop had the full mandate of Rhodesians inside Rhodesia. He had Ian Smith's mandate no doubt, but we had a feeling that what Ian Smith had done was part of what he was expected to do by South Africa. We had always said that wherever South Africa saw its interest, *our* interest must lie in the opposite direction.

Intelligence was making it clear that, by the time Mrs Thatcher came to power, you were supporting Mr Mugabe with funds.

That would not be quite right. We were supporting both. What we wanted was a coming together of the two forces of Nkomo and Mugabe. You may have heard a story, it's been exaggerated at times, that I gave both of them a pistol and said, 'Look! Fight it out!' It wasn't quite as bad as that! However, I said to them, 'Look! We believe in the principle that Rhodesia must be ruled by the majority. You are behaving like dogs in the manger. If you're not going to work together, maybe I should give you each a pistol and then you can have a duel. Whoever wins, we deal with him!' But, we supported them both. We allocated funds to both. We were a supporter of the external forces.

What led you to wield that club of an economic boycott, immediately before Lusaka?

Before that meeting at Lusaka, we had taken certain steps to make it clear to the British government that we were not going to stand for a half-solution, or half-cocked measures, as far as Rhodesia was concerned. We placed the ultimate responsibility for the solution squarely on the British government. So, now we had taken some economic measures to bring it vividly home to the British government that we *were* indeed holding them responsible. We left what you might call the 'trump card' – the taking over of BP, its operations in the field, its exploration and its downstream operation of marketing – to the eve of the Lusaka Commonwealth leaders' conference. I believe that was crucial. In fact, we had gone beyond that. We had made a plan, if *that* did not send enough right messages to the British government, that we were ready to go a few steps further.

What did you plan to do?

The plan was, basically, what happened. It was supposed to be in 'doses', of which one 'dose' was BP. We knew from our studies that we kept over half a million British workers at work through imports from Britain. We were ready to do something about that. We could have stopped importation from Britain. That would have meant another half a million unemployed.

So, the coercive threat you were able to apply to Mrs Thatcher was that the whole of Britain's position in Nigeria, its most important trading partner in black Africa, was in jeopardy, and you meant to carry that into effect?

Having fired the first shots then, obviously, carrying through the consequences would be no problem.

Lord Walston, in the House of Lords debate on Rhodesia in July, very shortly before Mrs Thatcher made her statement in Canberra, said that Britain had not been allowed to tender for one very large and important contract worth five hundred million pounds, because *of the Prime Minister's statement in Canberra.*

That is true. We *did* prevent British companies from tendering for contracts and supplies. As I said, we laid out a plan, and it had just started to unfold. The British government was angered by our action, and at the same time realized that the time had come when they must move along the line. President Kaunda told me that when Mrs Thatcher arrived in Lusaka, before the measures we took had been announced, she had given President Kaunda to understand the British were not going beyond the mandate they had for Rhodesia in the British general election.

'I will not be bullied,' she said.

Yes. 'I will not be bullied.' But, I believe Nigeria's contribution to her change of mind was substantial. We had intended to take a strong position. I had never met Mrs Thatcher, and I wanted to impress our intention on somebody who knew her, and the sort of person she was. That opportunity came with Malcolm Fraser's visit. I believe that Malcolm Fraser, who came here on his way to the Lusaka conference, and with whom I had a real heart to heart discussion, helped her to move in the direction that we eventually did.

Long after these events, you wrote a letter to the Financial Times *in London, in 1986, in which you expressed views about 'Mrs Thatcher's instincts being at war with her logic'. What bearing do you believe that may have had at the time?*

Those who know her very well have said that her first instinct is always wrong. She needs strong persuasion, a really strong person, to persuade her to another, and *right*, instinct. I believe that is what happened at Lusaka. Her first *instinct* was wrong. I have no doubt about that. But she was persuaded, and she took the right decision. I believe she has no regret for what she did. One must praise Mrs Thatcher. For a political leader to change his, or her, mind in the face of reality is a mark of statesmanship. I have tremendous regard for her.

Nigeria's move in taking over British Petroleum's operations was a dramatic but, somewhat quixotic, gesture. Actually *doing* it removed the *threat* to do it, as a bargaining counter in the Lusaka diplomacy. In that respect the Nigerians had fallen on their own sword, blunt instrument that it was.

In the diplomatic arts, as in many other respects, one gets on better standing up than lying down. Lord Carrington's disposition to affability was sorely tried by the Nigerian action and, on receipt of this Parthian shot, he erupted in the manner General Obasanjo has described. Among the controlling factors in formulating Britain's Rhodesia policy for the Lusaka meeting, was the sapient diagnosis of the Foreign Office that Britain was vulnerable to economic reprisals led by Nigeria. Therefore, what view had **Lord Carrington** himself taken, of the importance of black Africa to Britain?

Economically, it was very important – as indeed South Africa was. Nigeria, particularly, was a vital market. It was important that we should make absolutely certain, if we could, that we did not alienate an important market, and people who were friendly to us, whilst, at the same time, retaining our market in South Africa. That, of course, has been an extremely difficult thing to do. All this came to a head at the Commonwealth conference in Lusaka, in 1979, when there was the likelihood that there was going to be either a break-up of the Commonwealth, or such a division of opinion that there might conceivably have been sanctions against the British government from the black Africans.

Therefore, in searching for the reasons why the Conservatives, in office, changed their mind about Rhodesia from the policy of the election manifesto, how decisive was the threat that a country like Nigeria could make?

I don't think that was the main reason; that was a contributory factor. But, certainly, I must make it clear I hadn't changed *my* mind, because I never agreed with that in the first place! No, I think that the real reason why the Lancaster House conference came off was not so much that there was a sanctions problem in addition to everything else; it was the fact that the Muzorewa election was not really a proposition which anybody would have agreed to. Certainly not the European Community. Certainly not the Americans – at that time it was President Carter. Certainly not the neighbours. The only country that *would* have accepted that particular solution was South Africa. My view was that, if you went ahead on that basis, you would not end the civil war. You would have very much more involvement by the Soviet Union and, probably, by the Chinese, because they were supporting Mr Mugabe. We would have been much less likely to get a solution, and much more likely to get more problems. Therefore it really wasn't a practical proposition to accept it. That's what I thought.

Specifically on the threat that Nigeria could mount against Britain, of retaliatory commercial action, General Obasanjo, then the head of state, recalls that your response was volcanic when Nigeria acted, and nationalized BP.

Well, it was pretty provocative, on the first day of the Commonwealth conference, for the Nigerians to nationalize BP in Nigeria. That seemed to me to be an inexcusable thing to do and I said so. I also remember saying so to the poor Foreign Minister who, I discovered later, had no idea that this had been done and couldn't think why I was so angry! If I *was* 'volcanic' about it, then I would also be volcanic if it happened again. I think it was an absolutely inexcusable thing to do.

Nigeria's action, announced just before the talking was due to start in

Lusaka, seemed likely to make good the gloomiest of advice available to Lord Carrington, that there was going to be 'an almighty bust-up'. His diplomacy had begun, it may be thought, in a blaze of defeat. If, in consequence, there were few illusions left, there was as yet no major battle won, or lost. The Prime Minister and Foreign Secretary went off to join the great huddle of Commonwealth leaders, accompanied by their advisers. Among them was **Sir Michael Palliser**, the Head of the Foreign Office.

No one quite knew *what* we were heading for, in terms of the eventual outcome. I do not think any of us expected that we would witness the spectacle of the British Prime Minister and the Zambian President *dancing*, in most friendly fashion, on the closing evening of the conference and in a mood of great euphoria. We thought that there might well be an extremely difficult conference, and that it might result in the Commonwealth collapsing. There are differing judgements about how much that would matter, but I think all of us felt that if it collapsed around a problem like Rhodesia, it would matter quite a lot. The Prime Minister, when convinced of certain things, is never behindhand in grasping nettles and getting on with it. I think this is the conclusion she and Carrington jointly reached about the need for a political settlement. There is no doubt that when they came into office, in 1979, they began with different assessments of the situation. But, one should not underestimate the extent to which those two operated as a team throughout all this process.

At this stage, a political settlement did not mean, *at all*, acceptance of Mugabe and Nkomo as the future rulers of what was still Rhodesia. It *did* mean acceptance of a proper negotiation, to achieve a proper settlement. I, personally, think that she still hoped that she could produce a result along the lines *she* believed to be right, and I do not say that Lord Carrington did not *hope* for that.

So, there were still unresolved differences between them, about the underlying objective, on the plane on the way out to Lusaka?

There were differences in approach, in attitude, in how to handle it. I think there was probably agreement on the underlying objective. I think the differences were more in the assessment that each made of what was feasible. There, you could say, Lord Carrington took a more pessimistic, or realistic, view: partly, perhaps, because he knew more about the problem than she did. The Prime Minister did not really know very much about Africa at that time. Carrington knew quite a lot. That played a part.

Always there was the central thrust of the Foreign Office advice that Rhodesia should not stand in the way of the wider British interest. Judgements might differ as to how much it would matter if the Commonwealth disintegrated, but were agreed that 'if it collapsed over Rhodesia, it would matter quite a lot.' In consequence, any prospect of Britain taking the lead in recognizing Bishop Muzorewa's government had rapidly receded. How then, did the Bishop himself see his situation as the Commonwealth leaders assembled in Lusaka?

Bishop Abel Muzorewa was Prime Minister of what was now deemed to be Zimbabwe–Rhodesia and he had been the clear victor, following an impressive turnout, in elections which virtually coincided with Mrs Thatcher's own. These elections were held, in the middle of a guerrilla insurgency, between 17 and 21 April, 1979. Eighteen out of 932 polling stations were attacked. More than one and three quarter million out of a possible two and three quarter million votes were cast. The Bishop emerged with a 64 per cent majority of the votes cast, and with fifty-one out of the seventy-two black seats in parliament. This election was the one adjudged to be 'free and fair' by Lord Boyd before the Conservatives took office. The Foreign Office advice to the Prime Minister was that this 'internal' settlement of Ian Smith's would not end the war. Further, the terms of the new constitution had been designed to give the white minority a sustained, perhaps controlling, influence which stopped short of both the famous five principles originally established by the Conservatives,[10] and the British pledge, sanctified over many years, to majority rule. This, together with worldwide non-recognition of the outcome – the Bishop as Prime Minister of a predominantly black administration – more or less ordained that there would be no room for Prime Minister Muzorewa at the meeting of Commonwealth leaders in Zambia. To avoid provocation of those determined to be provoked, **Bishop Abel Muzorewa** was not invited to Lusaka.

Naturally, I was disappointed that we were left out. My understanding was that they did not want to include me, for fear that the people who were insisting that the Patriotic Front should be included might be offended. Therefore they decided to leave me out.

What was your reaction when Mrs Thatcher conceded at Lusaka that the Rhodesian constitution, under which you had been elected, was defective in

10 Unimpeded progress towards majority rule; guarantees against retrogressive legislation; immediate improvement in the status of black Rhodesians; an end to racial discrimination; and the acceptability to Rhodesians as a whole of any settlement. Labour added a sixth: that there was to be no oppression of one race by another.

certain respects, and then went on to speak of the need for 'genuine *black majority rule?'*

I did not like the reference to 'genuine black majority rule' because I believed that it *was* genuine black majority rule. The constitution? There is no constitution which does not have *some* defects. Although we had some in our constitution we had the hope, like any country, that we were going to work on perfecting the constitution. I believe that history will say those people judged us harshly, who felt the whole government, and a new situation, must be rejected because the constitution was not to *everybody's* expectation. I repeat, we were judged harshly on that point.

You described Lusaka, at the time, as 'an insult to the electorate and government of this country'.

Yes. It was. That I think is what I have already said.

Mrs Thatcher pointed out, at Lusaka, that British recognition, withheld despite your hopes, would not have helped much because a unilateral recognition, supported only by South Africa, would have made the war worse.

She did say that, and I believe that there is some truth in it: because the front-line states and the Patriotic Front would have ganged together and said, 'Now, let's continue to fight!' But, I want to be frank. That situation would have been short-lived. I have it on record that a lot of messages were coming out, from the Rhodesian boys and girls in the fighting zones, saying, 'What are we still fighting for?' There were beginning to be larger numbers of people accepting the offer of amnesty. So, to be sure, the Patriotic Front *would* have intensified the war – as they did. But, I do not think that would have been for ever.

You are saying that the delay by the new British government in recognizing you, at a crucial moment, actually removed the possibility of the internal settlement succeeding?

Yes, it made it very difficult for us to do what we needed to do, and what we had hoped and wanted to achieve.

In war, however, clubs are trumps, and Lord Carrington and his advisers took a different view of the durability of Mugabe and Nkomo's guerrilla forces. This reluctant, but calculated, diminishment of the Bishop, was to the advantage of the Patriotic Front. They were concentrated in their sanctuaries in the front-line states – Robert Mugabe, the leader of ZANU, in Mozambique, which bounded Rhodesia to the east and north;

and to a lesser extent – because his forces, although strongly assembled, were doing less fighting – Joshua Nkomo, of ZAPU, in Zambia, to the north.

Nkomo is a father of African nationalism; a huge man who was a product of the mission heritage and a contemporary of others like him who had long since become leaders of independent states: men like Kenneth Kaunda in Zambia and Hastings Banda in Malawi. As the acknowledged leader of the warrior Matabele tribe, Nkomo stood in a line that runs from King Lobengula, to whom, judging by photographs, he bears a remarkable physical resemblance, and from whom Rhodes had won the original concessions in Rhodesia.

Of the prospects created by the two elections in 1979 – the Bishop's, and Mrs Thatcher's – the victory of Bishop Muzorewa was dismissed by Nkomo as 'undemocratic' and his authority as illusory. There, it might be felt, Mr Nkomo's affection for democracy was coloured by the appetite for power. So, what, for him, was the significance of Mrs Thatcher's advent, with her disclosed preference of moving to recognize the Bishop? At this point, for **Joshua Nkomo**, the skies of metaphor remain unclouded.

I suppose you were once a soldier? You know that the strength of TNT is the resistance of the object? That's all there is to it. The strength of TNT is the resistance of the object that you want to destroy. That was just what we thought was going to happen, and it happened!

The TNT being the Patriotic Front?

Of course. If we had had the 'wishy-washy' doings of the Labour Party, who make you believe 'this' and *really* believe 'that' – whereupon nothing happens, then we would not have managed. But, with Thatcher, and those statements she made, we said 'Fine. Good. Now we are getting down to the *rock* regarding our country; and our dynamite will work better on this very strong rock, than on the wishy-washy policies of the Labour Party!'

But there was also another possibility, wasn't there? Indeed, it is what actually happened. It was the Conservative government that made possible a great change.

Because the rock was broken! Because the resisting rock got the blast. They *had* to change, and change in the right direction.

You were not a direct participant in the Lusaka conference. Did you have any great expectations of it being any different from a dozen other Commonwealth conferences where Rhodesia was concerned?

> We were not physically participants, but we pushed our ideas to them so hard that they were convinced the only thing to do was to support us. We had attended a number of conferences other than the Commonwealth, but the Commonwealth is different. They are much more involved, and much closer to our problems, than others. So we were very hopeful that our pleas would be listened to. And that particular conference was closer to the problem – just a few dozen miles from the border of 'Rhodesia', as it was then. You know, closeness to a problem makes a difference.

The guerrilla war was getting bloodier, as the heads of government congregated in Lusaka. Several hundred people a month were being killed inside Rhodesia, many more than in the neighbouring states. The guerrillas had steadily extended their control over Rhodesia's rural areas. Bishop Muzorewa's multi-racial government was bearing an almost impossible military burden.

Lord Carrington, who believed that 'time was running out', had in fact been advised that Rhodesia was on its beam ends, and capable of lasting only another few months. The Bishop's immediate objective – winning recognition, with its attendant prospect of ending the war – continued to elude him. However, having failed to prevent, or seriously disrupt, the elections which brought forth the Bishop as Prime Minister, how, at this stage, did the Patriotic Front measure the progress made towards its own maximum objectives? Most of the fighting was being done by forces based in Mozambique under the political leadership of **Robert Mugabe**, who is today the President of Zimbabwe.

> Of course, the ultimate objective, always, was the establishment of a democratic order, which would be just, and therefore must contain the salient principles of our own political thinking. The *immediate* objective was the overthrow of the system. Our liberation struggle had progressed to the point where we believed we had more than two thirds of the country – not 'liberated' as such, but affected by our operations in one way or another. We had liberated zones, we had semi-liberated zones, we had zones that we were contesting and we had areas that were yet to see our own operations. I believe that we had the rural areas in our grip. That made it easier for us, not so much to *dictate* our own position, but at least to win the objective of that ultimate readiness, on the part of our opponents, to establish the goal of democracy in the country. When Lusaka came, all that was the environment – and Ian Smith was ready to talk.

But would you agree that while you had made many advances, as you've just told me two thirds of the country was being affected to a greater or lesser extent by decisions that you *were making, you were still well short of ultimate victory. That was not in prospect?*

That is the point I was going to make. The end of 1979, with the coming of the rains, was going to see the development of the *urban* guerrilla struggle. We never got to that stage at all. Whether we regret that now is another question – but, at the time, we *did* regret that the conference[11] had come too soon. We did not agree with the Presidents of the front-line states, who attended in Lusaka, that the time was then ripe for us to have a political settlement. We felt we needed yet another thrust, and in the urban areas, in order to bring the fight home to where the whites had their citadels. But this did not occur, and I'm glad it did not, because it would have caused a lot of destruction in urban areas.

With Lord Carrington doing all he could to encourage the belief that '*everybody* needed an agreement', Robert Mugabe did not *want* one at Lusaka. The time was not ripe. Time, he believed, was on his side. He was convinced that a revolutionary overthrow would, in the end, be his, and that he was going to win anyway. The have-nots of Mr Mugabe's ZANU knew what they wanted, and it was the earth!

The Rhodesian response in this period of 'fighting to negotiate' was to raid with increasing severity the guerrilla sanctuaries in Zambia and Mozambique, states which were facing economic ruin. This helped give rise to that unpredicted constellation of common interests which formed in Lusaka among the Commonwealth leaders and Rhodesia's near neighbours, and which finally led to the settlement. The long-suffering hosts to the guerrillas of the Patriotic Front *did* want a settlement. At this juncture, unlike Mr Mugabe, **Joshua Nkomo** was disposed to heed them.

One has got to remember these things. In a guerrilla war, you usually fight from other people's countries. No matter how much they co-operate with you, all the time you feel, 'We are hurting these people. Their economy is being disturbed, their normal life made impossible.' You *feel* it. They don't have to say so, but you *feel* it. So we felt that. We felt that the war had gone on; that it had achieved its objectives, and that the British felt talking was necessary. We believed that if *we* moved, it would assist the countries that had suffered so much for

11 The constitutional conference at Lancaster House.

our cause. The constant reminders, and reminding oneself of that is, in itself, a burden to the person concerned.

As the pressure from the front-line states grew upon you for the reasons that you've given, is there anything that stays in your mind? You must have talked to Kaunda about the distress in Zambia. Is there anything you particularly recall about your exchanges with him?

Not so much the exchanges with him, but what happened, in Zambia, when the young people, refugees, young boys, were bombed. You know Kaunda, and how he is affected by things like that.

He's a very emotional man.

He is a very, very emotional man. He could not talk for a day or two. He was disgusted. And, you know, it hit me very hard also. Very hard indeed. There was a second bombing. The Smith–Muzorewa regime destroyed a camp, which we called 'Works Camp', where we repaired our trucks. This camp was near a home – a young couple's beautifully built little home. They had just spent all their money building it. It was demolished. Fortunately they had just left, two or three hours before, or they would have been killed. And you stand there, imagining all that, and seeing the thing flattened, when the young couple had just married, and they had worked so hard to build a little home. You feel very bad. All these things do come to me from time to time. Things like that don't get out of my mind.

In August 1979, Mrs Thatcher stepped from her plane, under the hot sun of Lusaka, into this landscape of competitive violence and obscure, eleventh-hour political possibilities – and into an even hotter reception. In an excited press of people, with the rest of her party battling to prevent themselves being isolated, she was at once borne off to a place apart and vigorously interrogated. Using the airport as a preliminary stage, black Africa promptly began to act out its diplomacy towards Mrs Thatcher's presumed intentions. **Kenneth Kaunda** had determined that she should be impressed, from the outset, with the hostility these aroused.

When she came she was confronted by our press men and women, at the airport. I don't think she has ever forgiven us for that!

It is said that she was 'captured'?

Ha, ha! So she says. We did not capture her. We would not capture your British government. No thank you. Seriously, however, our boys and girls asked her questions which, to begin with, she did not want to answer. But, I think she saw that it was right to say *something*. Of course, what she then proceeded to say, did not make us any more comfortable than we had been with what she said in Canberra! But, in fairness to her, when we began discussing these matters seriously – especially, I think, with the influence of Peter Carrington on her – in this very room, we began to see her start accepting the concept of a London conference on Zimbabwe. And, this began to change things.

You mentioned that all this was taking place in this study in which we are now sitting. When it comes to the relationship between Lord Carrington and the Prime Minister, what stays in your mind?

I remember one incident clearly. She was sitting alongside Peter Carrington over there, I was next to her, on her other side, and Malcolm Fraser, the Australian Prime Minister, was in the chair here.[12] I was chairman of the main summit, but we asked Malcolm Fraser to chair this committee of the Commonwealth summit, because we thought that as he was a Tory, Margaret Thatcher would feel more comfortable with him in the chair!

It became quite clear that the rest of us in the room were saying that a London conference on Rhodesia was the thing to go for. She was saying that she had pledges she had made, and which she would honour. I believe she meant by that the Tory conference pledges. But, at that juncture Peter Carrington said, 'Prime Minister, it would be a good idea for us to think about this.' And *she* said, 'All right, we will think about it.' That, I think, was a turning point. When we met next,[13] she was saying that she 'would have to think about this properly in London'. We thought that was a shift. It was good enough, I think, to enable her to get out of this room with honour! Also, in getting out, give her a chance to think about it all, seriously, and in a calmer atmosphere. So, that is how it all began to go.

What, essentially, helped create this 'atmosphere' conducive to agreement in Lusaka?

Well, we were not really *fighting* her. We were putting, I think, reasonable points. The whole lot of us. That is, Malcolm Fraser, Julius Nyerere,[14] Michael Manley,[15] the late President Zia of Bangla-

12 The President's little office is arranged with four or five armchairs drawn close together around his desk.

13 Meetings were of course frequent during the course of the conference and traffic in and out of Kaunda's study considerable.

14 President of Tanzania.

15 Prime Minister of Jamaica.

desh, Sonny Ramphal, the Secretary General of the Commonwealth. So also was the Prime Minister, and Peter Carrington. So was I.

We met in this room several times. The atmosphere was quite calm. Each time we discussed these matters we went back to the main 'summit', and explained what was taking place. There was quite a lot of activity, day in day out.

How aware were you that the United Kingdom needed your *co-operation, in order to emerge from Lusaka with anything like a plausible agreement?*

All of us were conscious of that. That is what I am saying really. We were not aggressive, we were not *denouncing* her or anything like that. We were merely making suggestions, and pointing out the dangers.

No doubt it is easy to exaggerate or sentimentalize the importance of such things, but the intimacy of President Kaunda's small study, with the senior members of the Commonwealth gathered there so closely, can hardly have failed to influence the minds of the participants. Anyhow, it was in that room, with the bookshelves behind Kaunda's chair lined with unopened, indeed uncut, pages of the voluminous works of Lenin,[16] that Zambia's President recalled 'a turning point'.

As Lord Carrington and the Prime Minister had intended, it was the Commonwealth leaders who had *asked* for a constitutional conference. This was the card Mrs Thatcher had come to play, even if the British had still hoped somehow to try and see Bishop Muzorewa through.

It was Mrs Thatcher's first Commonwealth conference. Nothing 'propinks' like propinquity! It was 'with the family assembled', as it were, in President Kaunda's study, that Mrs Thatcher appears to have completed her conversion over Rhodesia – in accordance with the persuasions of the Foreign Office, headed by **Sir Michael Palliser.**

Margaret Thatcher and President Kaunda actually got on very well. Of course he, perhaps, as she does, tends to be more excessive in public than in private. If you have a private conversation with Kaunda it's a very civilized, reasonable, sensible experience, because he is a civilized, reasonable and sensible man. The same thing is true with the Prime Minister. I think both of them tend to get a bit carried away in public. In that sense, I think she was probably pleasurably surprised by the reactions of a number of the Africans whom she met, and others whom she met, in Lusaka.

The deepest instinct of the British is for 'continuity'. The nation,

16 As I was able to see for myself while waiting for the President.

perceives itself as never acting more freely, or innovating more boldly, than when it is 'conserving'. While several strands of thinking in Britain have come to see it as an inherited burden, tinged with obsolesence, 'the Commonwealth' had put a hard-headed case to the Prime Minister. As **Sir Michael Palliser** makes clear, Mrs Thatcher had been impressed by that at Lusaka, and by the absence of modish hypocrisies from the African leaders.

> Although we tend to think of the Lusaka meeting as exclusively 'African', and obviously its main purpose was to try and lead up to a *Rhodesian* constitutional conference, it was also dealing with a lot of *other* Commonwealth problems which cut across the discussion on Africa. There was a full range of other things – the standard Commonwealth agenda – which tended to chop the Lusaka conference up a bit. That meant it was also a broader process of education for Mrs Thatcher in the nature of the Commonwealth.
>
> I'm not going to try and explain 'the nature of the Commonwealth' in thirty seconds, because 'the nature of the Commonwealth' is still totally ill-understood by most people, in this country and elsewhere. I would not pretend to understand it myself, completely. But there is no doubt that this was an educative process, more generally – and, not just in 'Africa'. I say this because I do think it played some part in a change in *attitude* by the Prime Minister towards the Commonwealth. There was a greater understanding of the value of the Commonwealth as an instrument, and as an organization: therefore, of the desirability of keeping the Commonwealth in play; of winning support within the Commonwealth for what we wanted to do in Africa – and in Rhodesia. Here again – it is the same thing – one should not underestimate the extent to which that influence operates on the *African* Commonwealth leaders. One of the extraordinary things about the Commonwealth is that, in spite of all the rows, and the fights, which go on every time they meet, there is a desire to keep the Commonwealth together. The heads of government *enjoy* meeting. I have got no doubt about that at all. Take a country like Pakistan for example, which has left the Commonwealth – but which *longs* to come back in. The Commonwealth is a strange animal, which does have this effect on people when they meet. You get some very sharp exchanges, yet there is a general feeling that it is a *valuable* coming together of people and ideas, and with a shared language. All that, I think, played its part.

Margaret Thatcher had had to take some very hard decisions in Lusaka. The Foreign Office had really led her to a change of mind in London, although that change was completed only in Lusaka. Once there, however, only she, together with Kaunda, could make Lusaka a success in the end. Goaded, as they had been, in the first instance, by the apprehensions which Mrs Thatcher had aroused, the outcome of Lusaka meant that the front-line states would now, in effect, have to *compel* the Patriotic Front, and the most reluctant of its leaders, Robert Mugabe, to take the constitutional path.

The very large diplomatic corps assembled in Lusaka, on the closing evening of the Commonwealth conference, rubbed their eyes in disbelief, as they watched one of the more spectacular reunions since Ulysses came home to Penelope, make it plain that Mrs Thatcher had returned to the fold. She and **Kenneth Kaunda** were the first to take to the dance floor.

Outside the conference hall we played another role. This is how the phrase 'my dancing partner' was born. We organized the ball. The band played some music – a song in one of our local languages here – called 'Margaret is a Good Girl'. I danced with her, and Denis Thatcher danced with Mrs Kaunda. All that was designed to create an atmosphere in which she would feel *comfortable*. It was among the factors, both in this community, and at the conference itself, which, I think, played some role in changing the atmosphere for the better. You should not forget, of course, the role that Queen Elizabeth played.

Which we must explore. But, a feature of Lusaka was this, if I may say, ostentatious rapprochement *between you, a leader of black Africa, and the British Prime Minister. You end up, by all accounts, addressing her as 'Dearest Margaret', and she calls you 'a dear sweet man'. How was such trust developed between you?*

Up till now, I have from time to time defied the wishes of the British Prime Minister on policies, but at no time – at least from my point of view – has that affected our personal relationship. For example, each time there is a tragedy in Britain I send messages of condolence. If she does something very good I say 'Well done Margaret!' Officially I say 'My Dear Prime Minister', *unofficially* I say 'My very dear Margaret'. She does the same with me. So, yes, we have maintained a certain relationship which is really very human.

But Lusaka was remarkable for what it did not *say. There was no condemnation of an 'illegal' regime. Unlike the OAU*[17] *resolutions, it did*

17 Organization of African Unity.

not call for recognition of Mugabe and Nkomo as 'the sole representatives of the people'. It did not make any conditions for the granting of independence which were not already implicit in the position the British had taken up historically. None the less, would it be true to say that because you expected so little from Lusaka, you were delighted with the outcome?

No doubt about that. But that did not come from nothing. We *all* worked for it.

President Kaunda reminds us that there were *two* very important British ladies at Lusaka. Among all the forces at work in achieving agreement there, Zambia's President volunteers the importance of the role played by the Queen. Elizabeth the Second is Queen of a great many Commonwealth countries. Even in those which are republics she is accepted, as head of the Commonwealth, in a formal sense. At Commonwealth conferences the presence of the Queen has a 'cementing' effect and there can be little doubt that the heads of state of the new Commonwealth attach great importance to their *own* relationship with her. Asked what view should be taken of the role played by the monarchy as the Rhodesian issue was finally coming to a head in 1979, the former Nigerian leader **General Olusegun Obasanjo**, makes the point.

As you know, all of us in the Commonwealth have a tremendous regard for the Queen. Her presence obviously gave hope. I don't know whether she whispered into any ears for the type of compromise that eventually came out of the Lusaka conference.

The monarchy, during the present reign, conducts what one senior Foreign Office official has described as 'the diplomacy of a thousand unspoken gestures'. It is a description which **Kenneth Kaunda** was happy enough to endorse.

I would go along with that! The Queen has many methods of influencing decisions for the right. I must say again, for the *right*. Queen Elizabeth, as always at these conferences, was a tower of strength for us. In this case she played a major role in the whole thing. First and foremost, leaders in the Commonwealth, of all sorts of different political thought, are agreed on one thing. They can *trust* her. So her role was that of a very effective mediator, in the sense that she listened to what thought was being brought to bear on the situation, from different corners. She was able to invite us to talk about this.

I do not know whether you are aware of how we organized Lusaka?

There were villas in one place, where all the leaders were staying. She stayed at the Lodge there. But she had two houses at the conference site, where *everybody* else was staying. One was her office during the day, and one was her rest room during the day. So we were able to go there, and discuss these matters with her. One by one of course. She was able to realize how things were going. It was of tremendous importance to us. She played that mediator's role very well indeed.

The discovery of the Commonwealth by the Prime Minister had a significant corollary – her discovery, at first hand, of the Queen's importance to the Commonwealth. The Commonwealth was, of course, important *to the Queen.* There had been an interesting moment, in London, just before the Lusaka conference, when it was suggested by the Prime Minister that the Queen might be advised not to attend, in view of the possible dangers to her personal safety. Buckingham Palace had announced, rather promptly, the Queen's firm intention to be there. Had the Queen been advised to stay at home, and whether such advice would have been constitutionally binding, authorities seem prepared to argue either way.

The influence of the monarchy is of interest as a contributory element, not just in the conduct but in the formulation of British policy over Rhodesia. In assessing the nature of the part played by the Queen in the Rhodesian settlement, would not her presence in Lusaka have made it more difficult for Margaret Thatcher to have pursued the line the Prime Minister had hinted at in Canberra, of trying to get recognition for the internal settlement and lifting sanctions? Among those who have given constitutional advice to Buckingham Palace is the historian **Lord Blake**.

I quite agree. I think that would have been extremely difficult. Even if it had been a conference without the presence of the Queen. Her presence, undoubtedly, did make it a great deal more difficult for Margaret Thatcher to adhere to what was, in fact, the official policy of the Conservative Party, and the party manifesto.

What might be said about the monarchy and Rhodesia, in historical terms? For example, in the beginning, how much had it been in sympathy with the policy of Cecil Rhodes?

Well, at that time it was Queen Victoria. She was quite sympathetic to him and rather admired his empire-building capacity. Indeed, she met him one or twice and got on rather well with him.[18] Rhodes's character can be endlessly discussed. Some of the things he did were extremely unworthy. Still, he was an idealist and the idealism did appeal to a very large section of the English middle and upper class and perhaps even the working class, in the last century. There was a great romantic feeling about it all. It was probably fading as the century went on, and that sort of world was becoming more remote. Certainly, there was a residual sense of that feeling in the very great sympathy to be found for Smith, in many quarters in England – and to a surprising degree – when he declared UDI. It is part of the reason why no government felt like killing UDI by force. It would have split the country too much.

Today, however, the present Queen is head of a Commonwealth which is shaped by the notion of mutual co-operation and the multi-racial ideal. In what direction did her sympathies lie and what was their influence on British policy?

It is a very difficult one to answer. The communications that take place between the Queen, or her personal advisers, and the Prime Minister – or other politicians – remain a closed book to historians for a very long while. We may have some idea what happened in the reign of George V, and perhaps even a bit with George VI, but we certainly do not know anything that has happened – not directly – in the case of the Queen's reign.[19] One can only surmise – and one understands, and one gets told by various people who do seem to *know* – that the Queen herself is very 'multi-racial' minded, and is by no means a believer in 'white ascendancy'. Very far from it.

The transformation of the Crown, would you agree, has in large measure been due to the Commonwealth outside Britain since the Second World War, and the assertion by most of the members of the Commonwealth that the Crown was indispensable to it? No alternative has been found to the Crown as the generally accepted symbol of the Commonwealth association. Of what importance will historians find that in explaining the eventual British policy towards Rhodesia, and the outcome there?

I think it is, probably, quite significant. The survival of the Com-

18 Legend records that at Windor Castle in 1891 the Queen asked Rhodes what he was doing in Africa and got the answer: 'I'm doing my best to enlarge Your Majesty's dominions' (Brian Roberts, *Cecil Rhodes* (London: Hamish Hamilton, 1987), p. 154).

19 The reign of George V was from 1911 to 1936; of George VI, from 1936 to 1952; and of the present Queen, from 1952 onwards.

monwealth, or the *preservation* of the Commonwealth, was really rather surprising, if you look back on the events that took place. The world looked as if it was going to head for independence for all the various former countries of empire, and a good many of them wanted to be republics. Therefore the whole question of the Crown as a symbol of loyalty was a rather difficult one to operate. It was one in the case of India, and India set the precedent for the rest. I think there is no doubt at all that the idea of the Crown, as a kind of symbol of association, has been very important indeed. It is a thing to which the Queen herself, by all accounts, attaches a great deal of importance, as indeed her father did also.

Is it true to say that the Crown could only fulfil this role because it had been transformed itself, in step with the transformation of the Commonwealth?

I think that is perfectly correct. It had adjusted itself to the changes. The monarchy has done so with remarkable skill over the years.

It seems fair to conclude that the presence of the Queen in Lusaka counted for much, and was made to count. The mounting scepticism in Britain about the value of the Commonwealth concept – which can be traced back to the aftermath of Suez in 1956, when much contumely had been poured upon it as 'a sacred cow' – was not enough to overgrow the ultimate fear of a break-up of the Commonwealth. More precisely, there was that decisive reluctance to allow it to collapse, as Sir Michael Palliser said, 'around a problem like Rhodesia'.

Lusaka produced an agreement whose fundamental character would only become more widely apparent as it was seen to underpin the emergence of a final solution. It was an agreement which was strong on flair and forecast. There was to be a constitutional conference, to be held in London, at Lancaster House. One last time, Britain was about to 'take up the white man's burden' and assume full colonial authority, and all the risks of such authority without real power. The British would supervise fresh elections. For their part, the front-line states undertook to deliver the Patriotic Front to Lancaster House. An essential element of Lusaka was the recognition that once there, it was up to Britain to *propose a solution.* This was a reversal of the previous efforts to settle the Rhodesian question by seeking American or United Nations involvement. Such endeavours had died lingering deaths, as with David Owen's initiative, when he was Foreign Secretary, at Geneva in 1978. This time, outsiders were to be kept outside. The British would have sole control at Lancaster House. Without that, of course, there could be no British leverage over the final outcome. Lord Carrington was able to leave Lusaka with this crucial British objective intact.

Recalling the Foreign Secretary's thoughts on his departure from London for Lusaka, and what he said was the 'general feeling that there was going to be an almighty bust-up, and that the Commonwealth would fall apart', could **Lord Carrington** lay his hand on his heart and say what he had *expected*, rather than *hoped*, to get out of the Lusaka conference?

What we went there hoping to get, was what we got. Agreement on the Lancaster House conference.

And, having taken this bold risk, which none of the Prime Minister's predecessors had taken, to assume full colonial responsibility, how important was it that you emerged, at Lusaka, with Britain's freedom to act?

Yes, that's right. That was essential. You see – to some extent this is hindsight, but I thought so anyway at the time – I believed that one of the problems which all the other solutions, all the other conferences, all the other proposals, had brought with them, was – the involvement of *other people* in the negotiations.

The Owen proposals,[20] for example, suffered very much for having the Americans there, and not because the Americans were not trying to be helpful. You not only had the Americans, you also had the front-line African states. The more people you involved in this, the more difficult it was to get a solution. I thought the only thing that you could try, which was novel, was to say: 'Look, it isn't any of your business, except the British and the Rhodesians, black and white.' Lusaka left us with that opportunity at the Lancaster House conference. We never allowed anybody beyond the front door there, who was not either Rhodesian or British. This greatly irritated all the front-line states, because they wanted to know what was happening. But it did make it very much more a family affair. If you could call it a 'family', at that time!

Lusaka had offered a glimpse into the murk, a flash from a light in the encircling gloom. But, as all parties now took themselves to London, in varying degrees of acquiescence and resistance, the fighting in Rhodesia continued.

For the participants, the journey from Lusaka, and other points in Africa, to the London conference was like putting down *Great Expectations* only to take up *Bleak House*. For, at Lancaster House, the hair-splitting and wrangling which fogs history was to occupy the next four months.

20 Constructed by David Owen, Foreign Secretary in the Callaghan Labour government, 1977–9.

And on the way, a determined effort was made, in far away Havana, to scupper the whole enterprise.

3

'Baa Baa Black Sheep'

Lord Carrington had won his gamble with reason in Lusaka. Having set out determined to pierce the heart of darkness, and to have done with the long rancour, civil and foreign, over Rhodesia, he had returned armed with the traditional British device for a transfer of power: the constitutional conference. This offered all parties an alternative to going on with the war. Britain was now committed to fresh elections in Rhodesia, in which all parties might take part, and thus to what Mrs Thatcher had called in Lusaka 'genuine black majority rule'.

The crucial element in the Lusaka communiqué was the acceptance, by the rest of the Commonwealth, that it was up to Britain to propose solutions. Lancaster House was not to be just another round of discussions with all the parties in Rhodesia. 'Once to every man and nation comes the moment to decide.' The purpose of Lancaster House would be to *decide.*

The vital importance of the free hand given to Lord Carrington for the London conference, becomes clear once it is realized that neither Bishop Muzorewa, who unless and until he was defeated at the polls was still the Prime Minister of 'Zimbabwe–Rhodesia', nor the Patriotic Front leaders, Robert Mugabe and Joshua Nkomo, were even close to accepting what had been agreed over their heads in Lusaka. Beyond the broadly defined objective of majority rule, faction seemed incurable. But, if either side in the war, or indeed other governments, had been allowed to alter or re-interpret the Lusaka agreement, the only likely foundation for a settlement would have been broken. So it was that almost every day, at Lancaster House, there were mountains to climb, corners to be turned, and importunities to be repelled.

Lord Carrington confronted the inevitable, and predictable, difficulty of giving general satisfaction. Not least to the eventual victor, now the President, **Robert Mugabe**.

I never trusted the British. Never, at all. I did not think they meant well towards us. In the final analysis, I do not think they wanted the liberation movement, and especially the one I led, ZANU, to be the victor. Their strategy was to get Muzorewa in, and perhaps excise part of the Patriotic Front, the ZAPU part led by Nkomo. They wanted to get it associated with the Muzorewa group, while we remained in the wilderness – as they perhaps thought we would – and then the rest would come back home, and form a new government. In other words, they did not want *our* victory. They did not want a Lancaster House success that would yield, a *ZANU* victory, but one that would yield what they considered to be the more 'moderate' side.

Lord Carrington and Mrs Thatcher had left Lusaka with the minimum British position secured. Carrington had sole authority to put up solutions at Lancaster House, and Britain would assume full constitutional powers in the search for a settlement. Without that Britain itself would have had no leverage. How did you view that prospect?

We never trusted the Conservative government to give fair play in regard to all political parties, and especially in regard to our own. We dreaded the fact that they were placed in such a strong position: a position they had never had before the Commonwealth heads of government conference in Lusaka and, what is more, with the support of our own allies! That was the predicament we found ourselves in. The British government had not shown any real determination to kill UDI here. We did not feel they *had* this will. We did not feel they had *acquired* any new will.

Those who had endured coercion now wished to apply it. Mr Mugabe, who considered his own position was improving the longer he carried his revolutionary torch into the Rhodesian countryside, therefore felt Lusaka had been a turning point reached too soon. He was intensely suspicious that it was also the wrong turning point. The British, as he says, preferred the appearance of equity and moderation to his own avowedly Marxist liberation 'struggle.'

'The essence of diplomacy is to get your own way' is an epigram attributed to Metternich. But with civil war hotting up in Rhodesia, Britain's Foreign Secretary had managed to do that only by limiting his ambitions. As **Lord Carrington** took up his stance of *realpolitik* over Rhodesia, how far did he consider that his diplomacy was up against Harold Macmillan's wind of change still – the tides of history – and that the radicals would win, in the end, as they had won elsewhere?

> Of course, the 'wind of change' was about twenty years before, but the winds had continued to blow rather strongly in those twenty years. You did have that history of war in Rhodesia, and the Unilateral Declaration of Independence. I thought that there was a possibility – and, certainly, those who were best informed in that part of the world at that time thought that there was a possibility – that the Muzorewa–Smith coalition would have much more support than, in the end, it did.
>
> Of course, there was also a feeling that the ZAPU[1] and ZANU[2] movements of the Patriotic Front would not necessarily hold together and that you might get a coalition between Smith, Muzorewa and Joshua Nkomo. All these things were mooted. I don't think anybody really knew. The first time it became apparent that that was unlikely to happen was when, first of all, Joshua Nkomo returned to Salisbury and then subsequently when Mugabe returned to Salisbury. The enormous crowds that turned out there to welcome them, were an indication that the Muzorewa election had been misleading. They had voted for Muzorewa because he was the *only* black man they could vote for. Mugabe and Nkomo not being there, the Bishop was the substitute. The *really* popular people were Mugabe and Nkomo.

However shrewd some suspicions might have been, as Lancaster House convened, a haze of uncertainties hung over the nature of any likely solution. We have Lord Carrington's word for it that nobody really knew. Meanwhile, attempts to undermine the foundation laid at Lusaka had begun at once.

At a summit meeting of non-aligned nations in Cuba, which took place in the short interval between Lusaka and Lancaster House,[3] Robert Mugabe lobbied intensively for a resolution from the militant member states of the non-aligned movement which would repudiate the Lusaka agreement. In the more radical atmosphere of Havana, objections were raised by Mugabe and by Joshua Nkomo that British diplomacy at Lusaka had succeeded in diminishing the standing of the Patriotic Front and that, therefore, they should not go to Lancaster House. These objections were overruled, in the end, by the front-line states, whose leaders, like **Kenneth Kaunda** of Zambia, stood fast.

> All this led to the point where Julius Nyerere, and I, and the late Samora Machel of Mozambique, met in Cuba at the summit of the

1 Zimbabwe African People's Union, led by Joshua Nkomo.
2 Zimbabwe African National Union, led by Robert Mugabe.
3 From 7 to 9 September 1979.

non-aligned nations. We had a job to convince both Robert Mugabe and Joshua Nkomo to go to London. They were saying 'No'. They were going to continue to fight. We then said to them 'No. No! You must go and *prove* that the British government is not serious in this. Otherwise, we will take very strong steps against you.' In fact, it is not too much to say, we *turned on* the freedom fighters in Cuba. That shows you how much we were convinced there was reason for us to give the British government, especially the British Prime Minister, a chance to prove us wrong. It was not the other way around. We did not want to convict her before she was tried, so to speak.

That non-aligned summit meeting at Havana was described by Mugabe as 'very forthright', the political code for a very profound difference of opinion. So, one is right to infer that there was a rift on this issue between the Patriotic Front and the front-line states?

There is no doubt about that, no doubt at all. There *was* a great difference, because the Patriotic Front wanted to go on fighting. We said, 'Give the British government a chance to prove that they are sincere in what they are saying to us.'

What was the essence of the pressure you were able to apply to Mr Mugabe, to make *him conform to your view of what should happen?*

Well all three of us, Julius Nyerere, the late Machel, and I, were saying, 'There can be no way we can go on like this', and they knew that. They were dependent on us in order to continue that fighting. If we said 'no' to the fighting, it would be 'no'. There would *be* no fighting.

When word of Mugabe's lobbying in Havana reached Nyerere and, in particular, Machel, who had been in Lusaka as an 'observer', they had confronted him in the face-to-face meeting which Mugabe himself described as 'forthright'. Mugabe had taken his stand on the OAU declaration that the Patriotic Front was the 'only legitimate' representative of the people of Zimbabwe. The front-line leaders, who were the major supporters of the Patriotic Front, were now committed to free elections and a constitution with safeguards for the whites. They told Mugabe that he should suffer no illusions that the Patriotic Front did, in fact, represent 'all the people' and, in addition, they sought to disabuse him of the notion that the OAU description of the Patriotic Front as 'the only legitimate' heirs of all Rhodesian aspirations meant what it said. Rather, it had been a device to discourage other African states from recognizing Bishop Muzorewa as Prime Minister.

In short, the threat from the front-line states was that, had Mr Mugabe refused to go to London and explore the constitutional path, Rhodesia's economically prostrate neighbours would close down the 'liberation war' which was being prosecuted from their territories. Furious though he may have been at seeing the prospect of a Salisbury with 'the broken wall, the burning roof, and tower' undermined – as prescribed in the classical manner of revolutionary overthrow – Mugabe had no option other than to comply. He left Havana with assurances only: to the effect that, if the Lancaster House conference came to grief because of British perfidy, or Muzorewa's intransigence, then they would all go on with the war. The front-line leaders had hewed to the line marked out at Lusaka where the Commonwealth had formally rejected the Patriotic Front's demand that it be given power unconditionally.

A figure of critical importance in both Robert Mugabe's and Lord Carrington's calculations had come forward in Havana to put his stamp upon the final outcome. This was President Samora Machel of Mozambique, from whose sanctuaries along Rhodesia's eastern border Robert Mugabe's forces came out to fight. In this, the first of what would be seen as two crucial interventions by Mozambique's President, Machel forced Mugabe's hand and insisted he go to the conference table in London. It was a crucial underpinning of the choice with which the leaders of the front-line states presented **Robert Mugabe**, arising from their undertaking at the Commonwealth Conference in Lusaka.

We thought they were selling out. When we met them, in Havana, and they put the issue to us, that we should negotiate, and we should not insist on some of the things that we used to insist upon by way of principle, we said 'No', that this would not do. I remember Nkomo saying that these were some of the things he had suggested in the past, so why should they bring them up now? They wanted us to accommodate Muzorewa at the conference, and others, and previously we had said these could only come as part of the *British* team. The front line said no. They felt that would not be the correct approach.

In that meeting in Cuba, immediately after Lusaka, you were meeting in a place, Havana, and in an atmosphere, one supposes, that was more inclined to support you, and your ideological belief in the necessity of revolution by armed struggle, as Castro had achieved it. None the less, the front-line states remained firm about trying to settle it constitutionally. When you describe this meeting as 'forthright', what can you add to what we know about it?

The front-line states said we *had* to negotiate, we *had* to agree to go to this conference. There we were, we thought we were on top of the situation back home, we were moving forward all the time, and why *should* we be denied the ultimate joy of having militarily overthrown the regime here? We felt that would give us a better position. We could then dictate terms. But this other way, no. We had to meet with Ian Smith and Muzorewa as *equals*. We said no. I, personally, did not think that was right, and I said so. Nevertheless, we agreed to give the exercise a trial. But, at that time, I never felt it would succeed.

The tension between you and Machel at Havana is clearly going to be of interest to historians.

Yes. It was not that we quarrelled, but he took a strong position. So did I. I didn't think he was right.

Why do you think he denied you the revolution he had achieved in Mozambique?

No – we had always conceded that, by and large, guerrilla struggles do not ultimately transform into military victories, and that there must come a stage when you negotiate a settlement. We had already gone through the process of negotiation. There was Geneva in 1976. We had the Anglo-American proposals in 1977–8. Now there was to be Lancaster House. What we argued about was that, good though these exercises are, the *conditions* must be right for them. We should not have a repeat of Geneva, and a repeat of what always seemed to happen.

Eventually we got what we would have got by military victory except that, because we had not really overthrown the regime, we had to make do with certain stringent constitutional provisions and restrictions on our power. The major aspect of power, majority rule, had come and there was a government elected by the people of Zimbabwe. That government would, as you know, bring about the necessary constitutional changes later.

What was decisive, in your view, in leading Machel, the pivotal figure in this, the hinge on which the war turned, to insist that the constitutional path be explored?

I think there were two aspects. One, was the fact that the Anglophone countries which attended in Lusaka persuaded Machel that it was necessary for this constitutional conference to occur, and be given a trial, and that there were good chances of it succeeding. Machel was perhaps persuaded by that, in part. Second, was the fact that our war had taken so long. The Mozambican people felt the pressure. They wanted an opportunity to develop their own country. If we ceased to exert this pressure on them, by our presence and by way of the facilities that they extended to us, they would be that much more free. Their resources would no longer be diverted in part to our war. They would then have full opportunity to attend to the problems of their own social and economic transformation.

But, it is interesting that when you looked at the Lusaka conference you appear to have had no thought that it would lead to the dramatic results it did?

No, I really had not. And, I had occasion to say, well, we were wrong.

It was easier to count your blessings when, as in Lord Carrington's case, they were not too numerous. As an ally of the Lusaka agreement, President Machel of Mozambique delivered, in the end, more than the British had hoped. Machel claimed for himself a Marxist orthodoxy as a revolutionary leader of the FRELIMO movement, the inheritors of power in the armed struggle which followed the disintegration of Portugal's African empire. But, Machel was, in effect, withholding from Mugabe the kind of 'liberation' which the prescriptive texts of Marx and Lenin ordain – that 'ultimate joy' to which President Mugabe has referred.[4] Samora Machel was killed in the crash of a Soviet aircraft among the hills near the border between Mozambique and South Africa in 1986. His successor as President of Mozambique was the Foreign Minister and a moving mind in policy, **Joaquim Chissano**. In Maputo, President Chissano recalled the nature of Rhodesia's importance to Mozambique at the time Samora Machel, and Chissano himself, took their decision to apply to Robert Mugabe a decisive constraint.

We regarded the independence of Zimbabwe as a consolidation of our own independence, since the illegal regime of Ian Smith had been fighting alongside Portuguese colonialism against Mozambique. We wanted a Zimbabwe with which we could co-operate, a Zimbabwe which would be peaceful. For the economic development of Mozambique, we *needed* a peaceful Zimbabwe. More than that, we wanted a reliable partner. We had been together in the struggle for the liberation of Mozambique which, with the Zimbabwean liberation movement, we regarded as part of the liberation of southern Africa. We therefore thought that it was important that we continue to support them in their endeavours. Our aim had been to try and persuade Great Britain to take up responsibilities in Rhodesia. Even before Mrs Thatcher's administration, we had tried to persuade the previous British government that if they would take responsibility it would be easier to establish a dialogue between the liberation movements and Great

4 See p. 69.

Britain. Then, of course, Smith and Muzorewa and all the others would participate in this exchange of views in search of a solution. But Britain felt uneasy in accepting again the role of a colonial power. However, we thought it was worth it, because the most important thing was to correct the mistake made in allowing Smith to proclaim UDI. That, then, was what we were trying to do in all the corridors around Lusaka. To create confidence in everybody. To show that we wanted peace and a peaceful, *negotiated* solution. We had this second role which was to encourage the liberation movements, who were very suspicious. We had to point out to them, and to salute sometimes, the correct positions taken up by the British. So we worked very hard for all this. We wanted to maintain *unity* within the Patriotic Front, which meant the unity of Zimbabwe, and at the same time to show the whites in Rhodesia that they would have a chance – as proved to be the case.

But then, after Lusaka, there was the meeting of the non-aligned states in Havana. In Havana, what view did you encourage Mr Mugabe to take of the possibilities of a constitutional settlement?

In Havana, we had a meeting of the front-line states with the Patriotic Front, to encourage Mr Mugabe and Mr Nkomo to go to London. I may say that we could see some reluctance on their part to do that. They were not very confident about the outcome of Lancaster House. But on our analysis, we thought that the Patriotic Front had a very big chance to emerge with good results from Lancaster House *if they went there with one voice.* We knew that Muzorewa and Smith could not stand very firm because they did not have a coherent philosophy on liberation, while the Patriotic Front did have the support of the people. Our role, in Havana, was to encourage them to go, and to concentrate on the main issues which would be discussed at Lancaster House – that is, the transfer of power. We showed that the other elements were elements which could be settled *afterwards.* The question of the *elections* was paramount. The other things, like the army, the assembly points and all the other issues of principle they took with them, could come later.

However, there was tension over the future directions for ZANU, and Mr Mugabe, and the path that ought to be pursued. Mr Mugabe has spoken of those exchanges with the front-line states, and with President Machel, as 'very forthright'.

They were, yes. Very forthright. It wasn't a meeting with Mugabe alone. Nkomo was present too. President Machel spoke clearly about the need to concentrate on what was *essential*, in order to bring about a settlement, and to make use of all the gains of the struggle. It was necessary to take advantage of these gains, and to recognize that the British had decided to be reasonable. So this was what was said – with vigour – by President Machel.

Can you remember his words?

Let me try. No. I'm not too good at imitation. It was vigorous – and the meeting was long.

But Mr Mugabe had spent five years in Mozambique in the conviction that the only way Zimbabwe was going to get its independence was by armed struggle and a military victory. There would be defeat, for one side or the other, in the field. You were now advising him that there was another way, and that he should accept the opportunity of a constitutional settlement. Clearly, he was opposed to that. What was the essence of the exchange that he had with President Machel?

All the time Prime Minister Mugabe was here, particularly after he took over the direct leadership of the armed struggle, we always gave him, in our talks, the experience of FRELIMO during the struggle: that the struggle was indivisible: the struggle was not only military but diplomatic and political, and these three fronts should be taken together. We did not tell Mugabe that instead of armed struggle you *have* to talk. We said that, at the same time you fight with arms, you must also fight with other means. I think he knew this, but we encouraged him when hesitation would appear. We helped him to see that there were chances, whenever the British proposals showed that there was an opening.

When President Machel pushed Robert Mugabe through the 'opening', we need harbour no doubts that he spoke bluntly. Samora Machel was a soldier, not a diplomat.

The war in Rhodesia was, supposedly, being fought over the issue of majority rule. At Lancaster House the British were holding out the promise of a constitution which would provide it, unequivocally. There was no less a struggle for power, of course, around the conference table itself. Mr Mugabe, unlike the leaders of the front-line states, was totally disinclined to scrape a second fiddle while Lord Carrington conducted the orchestra at Lancaster House. However, the joint leader of the Patriotic Front, **Joshua Nkomo** – who, it was felt (as Lord Carrington has said), might join a coalition with Smith and Muzorewa[5] – voiced a somewhat milder mistrust of the British.

5 See p. 67.

We agreed with Nyerere and Kaunda that the British had a responsibility, because Southern Rhodesia was their colony, of bringing about independence in the country. Britain had rejected this, and resisted it, and thousands of people had died as a result. We felt that, while they had to take responsibility to facilitate the elections and the independence of Zimbabwe, they should not go further than that. We thought they would not be as fair as we would have liked. That is why we did not want them to come back, and to take up the role they did. We felt they should just do the legal thing of bringing the Prince here to officiate, and that the Governor, with his helmet and his feathers, should remain in his regal palace, and they should not take part in things where they might have a hand in something we would not like!

You didn't trust the British?

Of course we didn't.

There was that rift on this issue, between the front-line states and the Patriotic Front at the non-aligned summit in Havana . . .

Who told you that? (Laughter)

Do you deny it?

No. It was a feeling. A feeling of 'Now look chaps, you have done so well that the British are now prepared to go to the table, you must see that this succeeds.' You know how it is. One understood their position, this country suffered a great deal as a result of our being there. Poor Mozambique. It had just got independence, they wanted to consolidate and really take hold of their independence. But, they were engaged in our struggle, and they were anxious to see us through. That would help them, as well, you see?

As you know, Mugabe has described that Havana summit as a 'very forthright' meeting.

Yes, it was indeed.

What comes to mind, particularly?

More by Machel than by anybody else. Robert[6] was on the receiving end, (laughter) as he was working from Mozambique. You know, Machel called a spade a spade! He didn't go 'around' the issue. He said '*You've got to move!*'

6 I.e. Mugabe.

To summarize this particular period, why did the Patriotic Front fail in its arguments, at Havana, that the Lusaka conference represented a calculated diminishment of the status and the role of the Patriotic Front? Even that it was a manoeuvre to install Muzorewa in power by the British?

No, we could not say that, because we knew that the front-line states would not have done that to us. They knew more than we did. They had talked much with the British, they were very close, and they were certain that the move would be a genuine one.

So it was that the makers of fate assembled at Lancaster House, in London, in September 1979, their suspicions magnified by the wiles of British diplomacy and with the spirit of contradiction and faction abounding. The inharmonious delegations of the Patriotic Front, led respectively by Mr Mugabe and Mr Nkomo, together with those of Bishop Muzorewa and the unsinkable 'Smithy', sat down around the table to decide Rhodesia's future. As they were unable to agree, it was Lord Carrington's job, from the chair, to make clear what *he* considered to be the basis for a constitutional settlement. **Lord Carrington** was an old hand. In the packed attic of his memory were stacked certain experiences, upon which he drew in formulating his approach. He had negotiated in the past, as First Lord of the Admiralty and as Defence Secretary, with men such as Krishna Menon of India, and Dom Mintoff of Malta – men who were notoriously allergic to accommodation.

That was one of the reasons why I was rather anxious to keep Lancaster House as something between the Rhodesians and the British: because I had had six months of negotiating with the then Prime Minister of Malta, Dom Mintoff, on the question of the bases. That was not just a question of a British base but also a NATO base, and so NATO got itself involved. As a result of NATO getting involved, instead of one person being able to negotiate, and saying to Dom Mintoff, 'Well, that's all the money you're going to get, full stop!', before you knew where you were, one country, or another, had sent their ambassador into Mintoff saying, 'I think I could probably squeeze out another five or six million for you'! In consequence, negotiations went on, and on, and on. People interfered in them. I do not say they were not well meaning. I'm sure they were well meaning – but it was really not very helpful.

Carrington's own informed prejudices about how to run the conference were sustained by the long institutional memory of the Foreign Office. To the notion of exclusion, keeping outsiders out, was added a principle hammered out on many an anvil in the historical past. The conference should be 'progressive', otherwise it would degenerate into endless argument. **Lord Carrington** would therefore take it one step at a time. He was the referee, and he made the conference rules.

> First of all, that you do not allow anybody else in! That was the first thing. That way you kept it very much 'in the family'. Secondly, that you had to dispose of things in an orderly progression. Obviously, you could not say, 'I will agree on the Constitution', or whatever it was, '*provided* I agree on the ceasefire', or 'the method of election', or whatever it might be. I did not allow us to leave the constitution until we had *agreed* on the constitution. I did not get on to the question of a ceasefire, and all the rest of it, until we had done that. So we did it in stages. This was not very well received by those persons who thought that this was a rather tough and disagreeable way of operating. I had a bit of a rough time, sometimes, in trying to keep them to that but, after all, *we* were running the conference, and therefore I was enabled to do it that way. I think that is one of the reasons why it all worked, because once you got the constitution out of the way, and they all agreed, 'Yes, this is the constitution we are prepared to accept, if we accept all the rest,' they could not then come back and *re-open* the question of the constitution later on. That was important.
>
> This was, after all the last try – and I think it would have probably been the last try – to get a settlement which everybody would agree to, however difficult it might be. Supposing it had all failed, and one had not got a settlement? The British government would then have been in a much stronger position to have said, 'Look we *did* have one more try to get a settlement. We *did* try and get ZAPU and ZANU into a negotiation in which we would have an election in which they would take part. We failed. Therefore we have no alternative but to accept the Muzorewa–Smith government. I think that would *then* have made more sense.

The difficulty at Lancaster House was the anticipated one of bringing the conference to the point of decision. It would be as fruitless as its predecessors if major issues could be left, only to be re-opened at each stage. Carrington's tactics gave the conference a solid basis on which it could be carried forward. Inside Lancaster House, the position of the parties was far apart on every issue. Since they could not agree, Lord Carrington set before them, at all stages, the basis of a settlement.

Concerning the constitution, for example, Carrington's tactics were applied in the following manner. To carry the conference forward he needed to know whether both delegations – the Patriotic Front, and the

Salisbury delegation, led by Bishop Muzorewa and Ian Smith – could accept such a constitution. Mugabe and Nkomo said they could not accept it, until the transitional arrangements following a ceasefire had been discussed. Lord Carrington replied that the constitution must be decided first; agreement on the constitution, however, could be contingent on agreement on the pre-independence arrangements. The Salisbury delegation, meanwhile, had maintained that the *only* purpose of the conference was to decide the constitution. Whereupon, Carrington made it clear that the British government was committed to fresh elections and believed these to be the key to international acceptance of Rhodesian independence. On 15 October 1979 Bishop Muzorewa announced his delegation's acceptance of elections supervised under the authority of the British government. The onus was now on the Patriotic Front. Their concerns then became concentrated on the issue of land. Lord Carrington stated that Britain recognized that the future government of Zimbabwe would want to widen the ownership of land. By this time all the issues had been discussed exhaustively and Carrington asked for a clear response, all round, on the question of the constitution. Four days after Muzorewa's acceptance, the Patriotic Front announced that, if they were satisfied about the transitional arrangements, they would not need to revert to discussion of the constitution. The conference was then, and only then, allowed to proceed to the next stage: this time, of course, against a background of agreement on the independence constitution.

Thus, the British were not acting as go-betweens, running from one side of the table to the other with proposals and counter-proposals. At every step, Carrington presented to the delegations a text, at first general, then revised, the latter on the basis of 'take it or leave it'. He would advance with those who agreed.

These were the tactics which so irked the Patriotic Front in particular at Lancaster House, 'some persons' finding them, in Lord Carrington's words, 'a rather tough and disagreeable way of operating'. Tough and disagreeable though it might have been, it was how Lord Carrington drew the threads of what turned out to be the final settlement into his hands. **Joshua Nkomo** recalls an exchange he had with Lord Carrington about such methods.

They were 'spider' tactics.

Spider tactics?

Yes, I called him a spider. You know, a spider creates a round web and it parks itself in the centre. Then it darts out to pick up a fly. (laughter) That's what he was doing. (laughter) He did not like it when I called him a spider. I said, 'You are just sitting there. You *know*, *beforehand*, what Muzorewa, and the other people are going to say. Then, you want to meet us all separately, Mugabe and Nkomo, and so on, so that *you* know what *we* all think, with us not knowing even what our own colleagues think!'

But, he was remarkably effective. This was the agreement reached at Lusaka, it gave him this possibility.

Whether he got it from Lusaka, did not remove the fact that it was a 'spider' type of arrangement. It is easier to attack a victim if you can separate him from the rest and get him alone. What it meant, really, was that Carrington was sitting in the centre and darting to every side of his big round web, organizing the conference, and in a position to handle us all *separately*.

But, all the time, tying you together?

That's right, and really getting us moving in *his* direction. Caught in the web.

One quality of the statesman is that there is nothing he does not remark. **Lord Carrington** has an aquiline eye for the smallest gesture, and a highly developed feeling for atmosphere. His own disposition is to agreement, and the possibilities of that appeared to have been strengthened in his mind by his first observations of how the warring 'family' of Rhodesia were conducting themselves in the corridors of Lancaster House.

There were these people who had been fighting each other for years, and during the coffee breaks at Lancaster House you would find that they were all talking quite happily to each other. A lot of them had been at school together, they'd known each other for years and years, and there was good deal more affinity between them than you would ever have got if you had a whole lot of people from different countries taking part in the conference, and making it a very much more international affair. I think that atmosphere did create a feeling that, possibly, there might be a settlement.

It is known, isn't it, that Tongogara,[7] *Mugabe's military commander of the ZANU forces, actually went up to Smith at Lancaster House, and started chatting to Ian Smith about meeting Smith's mother on the farm at Selukwe, where he had once worked?*

7 Josiah Tongogara, who had been the fighting commander of ZANU (ZANLA) forces since 1972. He was killed in a road accident in Mozambique in December 1979.

Yes, but I saw a lot of that going on. I think that was an important thing in itself. There was a feeling that they all belonged to one 'close'.

There was 'a breathless hush in the close' as Lancaster House got under way. The British had succeeded in investing this constitutional conference with a sense of drama and finality. This would be *it*, for Rhodesia. This time, whoever miscalculated, or made mistakes, would pay the penalty. While Lord Carrington had no real power to deploy, he had two important levers at hand. If the Patriotic Front walked out, he would recognize Bishop Muzorewa, the so-called 'second class' solution. If Muzorewa walked out, Britain would refuse independence, and continue sanctions against Rhodesia. The threat to recognize Muzorewa was, in turn, a threat to the front-line states, who would exercise their influence to keep Mugabe and Nkomo in the conference. Bishop Muzorewa and, without doubt, Ian Smith, *wanted* the Patriotic Front to walk out, this being the only way the Bishop's government could achieve recognition. However, in order to stay on at the table in Lancaster House, the Bishop had to keep on making concessions. At the same time, little by little, caught in this same web, **Robert Mugabe** was being committed to a constitution he could not choose and did not want. But if Mr Mugabe had walked out, Lord Carrington's hands would be untied. Britain would then be free, as he has said, to call for recognition of Muzorewa.

They hoped, of course, that we *would* walk out. We were very much aware of that and it is why we worked hard, as ZANU, to prevent two things happening. One, in order to prevent ZANU and ZAPU falling apart we had to remain *together* as a Patriotic Front, and we made lots of concessions to ZAPU on certain issues as we discussed our own position. Secondly, as the Patriotic Front – ZANU and ZAPU together – we made sure that we would *never* walk out, never ever. We determined that whatever fight we were going to put up, to make it a fight based on our arguments, and that we must win through our arguments: and where we failed to obtain the absolute position – our own target – then we could always work out a compromise position. This is what we did right the way through.

We found Lord Carrington's strategy absolutely baffling and, in a way, repugnant. He would come to us with a position which had already been worked out between him and the other parties and say to us, 'Well, the other parties have agreed to this, so what does the Patriotic Front say?'

He was chipping away at your position all the time?

Yes, all the time. And the other parties *had* no arguments. Muzorewa, nothing at all! At one time I said, 'Oh look here, why even on a fundamental issue like land don't you say something?' You see, that was the main grievance throughout the war, *land, land, land.* Why should not Muzorewa be heard on it? At one time we had Muzorewa, we had Mundawarara, we had George Nyandoro,[8] to talk to on this question. I said, 'But you are *Africans*, how dare you accept that the position on land shall be governed by the Bill of Rights? We can't get anywhere with the Bill of Rights. Don't you remember your history? The land was never bought from us. Support our position on this one!' They said no, they could not. So, at one time I said to Lord Carrington, 'Look at them! What are they? Baa baa black sheep, have you any wool!' It took him time to unravel that but finally he got it.

It's taking me a bit of time to unravel it.

Well, it *was* 'Baa Baa'. They were black sheep, just saying 'Baa baa' to the master! You see? (laughter)

The land issue was, as you say, the central proposition. Yet, to many people's surprise you gave way on it.

We had to. That is the 'giving way' that I talked of, having to compromise on certain fundamental principles, but only because there was a chance, in the future, to amend the position. We had got the main concession on the creation of democracy. There would be democratic elections in the country, and if a government was going to be yielded up by those elections, based on majority rule, then that government would, in due course, bring about the necessary changes. So we didn't worry very much. But it hurt us. We did not like it.

Robert Mugabe, aiming sardonic taunts like 'Baa baa black sheep' at Bishop Muzorewa and his team, at once made a forceful impression on all his interlocutors at Lancaster House. The Bishop was no verbal gladiator. A nice man, with the best of political manners, he was sometimes too polite for words and so said nothing. Robert Mugabe's mastery of aim and object classed him, in the opinion of one senior Foreign Office official at the conference, as 'a starred-first intellectual'. That impression would take root among the British the further the conference progressed, and it influenced their thinking. **Lord Carrington** recoiled from the bitterness of politics. He entered them on the side of reason. Thus, intuitively, he discounted Mr Mugabe's professed revolutionary beliefs with their roots in the class struggle.

8 Dr Silas Mundawarara and George Nyandoro were both members of the Bishop's official delegation to Lancaster House.

I gave a dinner party for the delegation before we started the Lancaster House conference, and I said to him, you know, 'You were in jail for ten years. Are you bitter?' And he said, 'I'm not bitter against Mr Smith or against the white Rhodesians, but I *am* bitter against the system.' I thought that was an interesting remark. Indeed, I think that what has happened since has borne out what he said, and that what he said was true because he has never taken it out on all those people. After all, Mr Smith has still got his farm and is in Zimbabwe now.

He was not taken out and hanged from the nearest tree?

He wasn't hanged and until quite recently he was a member of parliament. I think that shows that it really was 'the system' which Mugabe wanted to change, and that he was not bitter against the people concerned. I think that was very magnanimous in fact.

Had you ever tried to meet Mugabe before his appearance at Lancaster House?

Yes, I had. I had tried to meet him when I was going round Africa on one of my trips. He refused to meet me at that time. I met one or two of his people, but he was the only one I had not met.

Is it true to say that we had no idea, that you *had no idea, how good Mugabe was until Lancaster House, and his performance at that conference?*

Oh, he had a reputation before that. I think that Mr Mugabe was the one who was least interested, personally, in the settlement at Lancaster House, because his people were doing all the fighting. He had a good deal of time on his side and he is a comparatively young man. All the others had reasons for wanting a settlement fairly quickly.

But was it at Lancaster House that you realized Mugabe was the chap we were going to have to deal with in the end, and until then you were still hoping for some Kenya-type of government?

Yes. I think that is probably right. I don't know whether it was quite as clear as that, but it probably was the direction in which it was all heading. Yes.

Is it right to suppose that we were working to exclude Mugabe from power, if possible, at Lancaster House?

No, not working to exclude him. But he was an unknown quantity, in exactly the same way that Nkomo was an unknown quantity and Muzorewa was more of a known quantity.

But Joshua Nkomo was hardly an unknown *quantity.*

He was an unknown quantity in terms of what he would do when he got there! He was, after all, the father of Zimbabwe nationalism. So I think there was a hope that you would get a government which was a known quantity and Mugabe was a very unknown quantity. I think Mr Mugabe was probably persuaded, to some extent, by Machel and by Nyerere to accommodate to some of the things at Lancaster House, which he obviously did not like.

Foremost among the things Mr Mugabe did not like, and over which he had seemed prepared to break up the conference, was the issue of land and who would compensate Rhodesia's white farmers for sequestration. Faces were saved at the last moment by an international fund for land development supported by the United States. Whereupon Mr Mugabe accepted the new constitution. A Bechers Brook had been jumped. Now, and literally to gasps from the assembled delegations, Lord Carrington gambled Britain itself. With fighting in Rhodesia intensifying, he disclosed Britain's intention to take over all executive authority, including control of the armed forces, while new elections were held. Bishop Muzorewa, convinced he was the legitimate Prime Minister by a clear majority vote cast only six months earlier, was now pressed by Lord Carrington to stand aside and *give up his authority as Rhodesia's first black leader* to a British governor, while another election took place. Getting the Bishop's agreement to do so was crucial to getting a settlement. For **Bishop Muzorewa** the decision he was called upon to make at Lancaster House meant exploring the city of the soul.

The fact that we were going to have another election, after we had been elected ourselves and in government for just six months, was a real crisis and a very testing time for my delegation and myself. Mr Smith was no longer a party to be reckoned with. Whatever Mr Smith did was not going to make an iota of difference to what *we* proposed to do. We had abolished discrimination over land and the only issue was its redistribution. What we did not want to do was say, 'Whites out! Give us the land. You are out!' Perhaps we were too Christian to be politicians, but we did not believe that we should do that. We pressed for the land to be acquired by legal process. Get it from the people who want to sit in London and say, 'I've got land in Zimbabwe.' Tell them, 'Sell your land to us because we have people here who want to use it and not just to grow grass.' *Buy* it from them, rather than *grab* it. If others wanted to take it in the revolutionary way, we did not agree with that. The Patriotic Front did not want white folks in Parliament. We reasoned that if you really meant to create peace and harmony for all you had to see that all were represented. Black and white.

When I came into politics it was by invitation. I at first refused, but people persuaded me to lead the fighting of the Pearce Commission proposals.[9] When I came in, my one objective was majority rule and a free country for all. When the Pearce Commission was over my only platform had gone. I went to Britain and down to speak in Trafalgar Square. I tried to talk to any official I could get hold of and wherever I went, to the UN, and in the United States, I spoke in favour of a constitutional conference because I believed it was the hope of peace and a new age for our country. So, when it was suggested we should have a new constitution and a new election, I considered it not in terms of my own interest, but in the interests of the country. I believed that if the new elections were fair, then we were certain to win.

How difficult a decision for you was your agreement to give up your office as the elected leader of Zimbabwe–Rhodesia during the transitional period before fresh elections?

It was very difficult, and it was very painful, because my objective was what was best for the country, not for myself. Let me repeat, I did not come to seek office, or seek power, I had been persuaded to join politics for the good of the country. However, since I had been elected as a leader I expected to do the things which I thought *were* for the good of the country. I wanted Zimbabwe to be one of the most democratic countries on earth. If some called me power-hungry it was in order to perform that task. So, it was very difficult for me to accept stepping down. For the sake of the country I did accept it. But, I had to go and persuade all my colleagues, the whole delegation. They thought that it was a terrible sell-out for me just to say, 'We accept and, in accepting, accept also that we are an illegitimate government' and all that. It was not very easy. To be honest with you, that was the hardest part of my stay in Lancaster House.

Can you tell me in what circumstances you took that decision? Did you take it in the end alone and by yourself?

Well, you are asking about the whole philosophical basis of how I make my decisions. All right. If I have a problem, and I have to make a crucial decision, how do I do it? What I do, is what I did over there, in London. I had to go quietly, usually very early in the morning, like

9 A Commission chaired by Lord Pearce had been established to inquire into support for Ian Smith's attempted settlement with Rhodesia's tribal chiefs. Pearce reported in 1972 a substantial African majority against.

four o'clock, or five o'clock, in the morning, and I try to listen to the universe. The Christian signals to God for guidance. Pray about it. Meditate about it. Get what I think is the spirit guiding, but not only that. Face the realities. Make a list of the advantages and disadvantages in deciding one way or the other. First of all, is it good for the people? Or is it just good for *me*, because I must put myself in the context of leading the people? Is it good for the cause? Those questions and answers. It must be good for the cause, not just good for Abel Muzorewa. A combination of that brings me to a decision. That is what I did in Lancaster House. Then I went in to convince my colleagues, and as I say it was not easy to convince them. In fact, for them, it was very heart-breaking. But we did it. Some have never forgiven me for doing that. They say we should have gone to fight, and fight for ever. I did not think we should just fight for the sake of fighting.

But praying for guidance as you were, I imagine in a London hotel bedroom . . .

Yes, of course. There was no chapel around (laughter) you don't pray in chapels all the time! Yes, right there. I could be just sitting, and quiet, in prayer you know.

But, praying for guidance in that London hotel, you must have realized that it was the end for you. In the sense that giving up power in Africa means that you never regain it.

Of course. I knew that. But remember the guiding principle was not myself.

The Bishop had found the strength to fail, and his decision was indeed the beginning of the end for him.

Samuel Goldwyn, the film magnate, once disclosed his prescription for success in winning the support of the mass audience: 'You begin with an earthquake and build up to a climax!' At Lancaster House, the climax was still several weeks away. Lord Carrington had begun, it might be said, with a diplomatic earthquake. The Bishop's agreement to step down marked the final eclipse of Ian Smith's settlement with the African leaders inside Rhodesia. For Ian Smith himself, Lancaster House was the end. There he fell, never to rise again. The fall of 'Smithy', that obdurate master of ambiguity, and the part being played by South Africa, the shadow to the south, has brought us to the last stages at Lancaster House.

4
'Goodbye, Mr Smith'

In this sudden grasping of the nettle and swirl of diplomacy in 1979, where was the hand of South Africa to be found, now that support for 'white supremacy' in Rhodesia had been withdrawn?

When President P. W. Botha of South Africa undertook to reform aspects of apartheid, he had described the predicament of Africa's Deep South in words which sounded muffled echoes of Patrick Henry's famous call to the Virginians: 'Give me Liberty or give me Death.' 'We must adapt or die,' said Mr Botha, which might be construed as 'Give me Adaptation or give me Death.' However, any adaptation contemplated drew the line at British constitutionalism as a solution to the thronging desires and impulses of black Africa.

The Afrikaaners had fought Britain for their freedom at the turn of this century. Having done so, they were not about to liberate the blacks by giving them the vote – and with it, power over the whites. Considering themselves also to be 'freedom fighters', the Afrikaaners had fashioned their own 'liberation theology' – apartheid.

The euphemism of apartheid, the entrenched belief that black rights cannot be expressed as 'one man, one vote' in a unitary state, which had evolved as the British solution for Rhodesia, marked a frontier between the British and the Boers as wide as the Limpopo, broad as any Zambesi.

In 1979, Britain had veered away from the policy declarations of the Conservative Party and Mrs Thatcher's government when it took office. British ministers, in their determination to make a final attack on the Rhodesian issue, had agreed at the Commonwealth conference in Lusaka, in August that year, that Ian Smith's achievement of a multi-racial government, supported and welcomed by South Africa, did not go far enough. South Africa's foreign minister, **Pik Botha**, recalls how the big shadow to the south then took stock of this shift in the British position.

Our point of view had been that it was a British issue and that Britain and Rhodesia must find the answer together. We would not interfere. That has been our attitude all along.

None the less, it was clearly a bit of a jolt for you wasn't it?

Quite frankly, we did not like it at all, and I told your ambassador that.

What did you say?

I told him that you were making a mistake and that the country itself was one day going to pay a heavy price.

I believe you used a rugby analogy, saying that it was as if one did not like the result of the game and wanted to replay it?

Exactly the point. Britain shifted the goal posts in Rhodesia and it's very difficult to kick a goal if the umpire's moving the goal posts all the time. The world is doing it now with South Africa as well.

However, what judgement had you formed at that time, in August 1979, of Rhodesia's ability to go on with the war?

In the first instance, that was an assessment Rhodesia had to make herself but, naturally, we had a fair idea of what it would cost. It became clear to us that although the struggle *could* have gone on, it would spill over into the region – and that is to say, *our* region. We are interested in *stability* in this region. You will remember that, in the seventies, Mr Vorster actually suggested to Mr Smith that the proposals then made would have ensured white participation in government for a considerable period. Those proposals would have introduced a gradual, evolutionary change-over in which black leaders could have taken part, and we believed, slowly identified themselves with the government in Salisbury. It would have been a gradual process before they became the majority, as a result of the standard of education of the blacks, and properly based on the attainment of educational training standards. We felt Mr Smith should have accepted that.

You say the war could have continued. But, it can't be wide of the mark to say that you knew, by August 1979, that the game was up for Rhodesia?

You must not forget that Muzorewa was then Prime Minister. So, from our point of view, there was a moderate black leader in charge. It appeared to us, and it appeared to me, from meetings I had in Salisbury with the Cabinet and with Bishop Muzorewa in the chair, that it all went well. There was a lot of potential in that idea of black

> and white partnership. It appealed to us and it looked good. There was an expectation that Muzorewa would win the election, eventually.
>
> *But, unless you took over the war, it could not go on? Rhodesia's resources were limited.*
>
> That might have been the wish of the Rhodesian leaders. I am not aware of any formal request to come before me, as Minister of Foreign Affairs, to do so. We could not take over the war then because Britain claimed sovereignty, and that would have brought us into a direct clash with Britain. A direct conflict with Britain was something which, in my opinion, this country could not afford.

Thus, South Africa, was also to be counted among those contiguous states which not only wanted, but needed a settlement. The Republic had been meeting Rhodesia's defence bill since 1976. By the first half of 1979 the bush war in Rhodesia was costing South Africa one million pounds a day. Ian Smith shared the South African belief that no accommodation was possible between the paramountcy of the African and what Cecil Rhodes had ambiguously described, when white Rhodesia's history began, as 'the rights of civilized men south of the Zambesi'.

But Ian Smith's Micawberish expectation that South Africa would feel compelled in the end to take over the war had dissolved. A ring of common interest in ending the fighting had been drawn around Rhodesia's warring parties, and was now virtually complete.

British diplomacy prefers to allow horses to fade in a long race rather than a short one. Ian Smith's race was run. The settlement to which he was so bitterly opposed allows him to live today in suburban tranquillity in the Salisbury which is now Harare. Mr Smith's bungalow is theatrically juxtaposed with the premises of that surrogate intruder into the destinies of southern Africa, Cuba. Over the garden fence next door, 'Smithy' is overlooked, indeed overtowered, by the sentinel presence of the Cuban Embassy, a veritable porcupine of aerials bristling on its roof.

As Ian Smith had set out in September 1979 for what proved to be his last battle with Britain, at the constitutional conference at Lancaster House in London, the whole tide of events was against him. At the end of all those talks, and talks about talks, that had been held down the years since his illegal declaration of independence, he had always taken up the same position. He had said it coming home from his encounters with Harold Wilson in the Mediterranean in the 1960s aboard HMS *Tiger* and later *Fearless*. Always, he had urged the waverers that the terms on which legal independence was offered to Rhodesia could be improved upon. But now, new men, strange faces, other minds were in a position to transcend his prejudices, in what was clearly likely to be a final effort to achieve a constitutional settlement. As many chose to see it, Rhodesia's newly elected Prime Minister, Bishop Abel Muzorewa, was tied to Ian Smith's fiery chariot. How many cards did **Ian Smith** believe he held at Lancaster House?

Very few. Because I had surrendered my position of responsibility in this country. I had done that at the request of our friends in Britain, who told me that this was the best way of getting a solution. They told me that if I did what I subsequently succeeded in doing, they believed that would solve the problem. So I did that. I then found myself in a position where I had surrendered my power and responsibility and the British government, once again, went back on their undertakings.

That is a moot point. The British government's diagnosis of your internal settlement was that the reality of power lay in your hands. Power had been transferred in name only to Bishop Muzorewa, as you held all the civil service commissions and power and authority over the armed forces.

But that was a distortion of the truth. Once the transition took place, and Bishop Muzorewa became Prime Minister, I was no longer in control. It was a fact that the armed forces then took their orders from the new Prime Minister. The same as happens in any democracy, once a party is voted out of power, I mean the civil servants no longer continue to have their loyalty to the government that has gone out. That is the democratic system, and that is what honestly, genuinely, took place in this country. There were no ulterior motives. We could not possibly have instituted something that was going to be a farce, or was going to be dishonest. It would never have worked. Our civil servants were brought up in the true traditions of the British civil service. Their loyalty was to the government they were serving. They were divorced from party politics and prevented from taking part in politics. Contrary to what has happened today in our country.

However, the general view, the view that came to be held in Britain, would you agree, was the one articulated by Lord Carver, among others. He was one of the many sent out here to Salisbury,[1] *in other years, in pursuit of a settlement. He said that there was 'a need for Bishop Muzorewa to throw*

1 By David Owen, Foreign Secretary in the Callaghan government. Lord Carver was the retired Chief of the Defence Staff and made several visits to Rhodesia in the course of 1977–8 at the time of the abortive Anglo-American proposals. With the Patriotic Front united in rejection of the Kissinger–British proposals, Owen essayed the notion of an interim British administration in Rhodesia, with Lord Carver as the 'Resident Commissioner'.

off that white parasol', which you had held over his head with your internal settlement, and which 'now protects him from the African sun.'[2]

Yes, but I think those were just words to suit the circumstances in Britain. He gave the answer which I think people wanted him to give. I must assure you that we believed that that was completely artificial.

How did you find that Lord Carrington's views differed from those put to you earlier by Henry Kissinger?

We were very disappointed in Carrington. There is no doubt that, at Lancaster House, for example, we were deceived by him. I am not the only one who would say that to you! Muzorewa and a number of other, impartial, Rhodesians who were there would say that to you. They were given one story by Carrington and he subsequently reneged on that. So, as far as we are concerned there is no doubt at all that he was the villain of the piece.

But you were desperate for recognition of your internal settlement by 1979 and, therefore, for the first time since 1923,[3] *the United Kingdom had a degree of influence over Rhodesia it had not had since then. How did you see your prospects at Lancaster House?*

The crux of the matter was that for the first time since I started negotiating with the British I was no longer in control. Had I *been* in control we would never have accepted Lancaster House. But that is how clever British diplomacy is. I was assured, by members of the British government, that if I came to the kind of agreement that we had made with black leaders who were in the country, an agreement which obviously indicated that we had accepted the philosophy of black majority rule – and let me repeat, that is exactly what the transitional government *did* – then, under those circumstances, they would accept us. We went to Lancaster House and found that they did not. Actually, the first time we were betrayed by the British was even before that, when we went to Geneva,[4] after the Kissinger–Vorster talks.[5] I was asked if I would go to Geneva to finalize an agreement and that it would probably take a week or so. My reply was that I did not have to go to Geneva to finalize an agreement, if all they wanted was my signature. I could give *that* to them here. But, if they did think I had to go to Geneva, 'just to sign', I would go there

2 In the House of Lords debate on Rhodesia, 10 July 1979.
3 When Rhodesia acquired self-governing quasi-dominion status.
4 The Geneva meeting was convened by Britain on 28 October 1976.
5 These took place in September 1976 in Geneva and as a consequence Ian Smith announced his acceptance of the principle of black majority rule.

for one day and come back the next. I was then told that, because of the people we were dealing with, it might take 'a little bit of time'. There would be 'problems' that they would have to explain to these people. So, 'Please', they said, 'be prepared to allow a week.' Well, I am a reasonable man – I always have been – and so I went. But it was very clear to me from the moment I arrived that what the British were trying to do was *change* that agreement. It was why the whole thing failed, in the end. Lancaster House was merely a continuation of that.

An analysis of Lancaster House, particularly of the British tactics in the first couple of weeks there, suggests that the British team spent that time trying to break you – Ian Smith – down. To isolate you from Muzorewa. To get Bishop Muzorewa 'out from under' you. Do you agree with that?

Oh yes! You are absolutely correct. And, of course, they succeeded in doing that. Carrington told Muzorewa that he would just ask him to pull out of the Prime Minister's office, but that it was going to be 'temporary'. In fact, he could 'leave his slippers there' so that they would be there when he came back, after the election. Unfortunately, that was how they took poor old Bishop Muzorewa for a ride. He was not a politician. He was just a simple man of the church. That was his rightful place. He did not understand the game. He had fallen in among a lot of international political sharks and they pretty quickly stripped him of everything. I warned him of this. Regrettably, he had been weaned away from me by Carrington, and in the company of the Foreign Office – who, as you know, traditionally, are some of the smoothest diplomats in the world.

Some of the exchanges you had with Lord Carrington were not very smooth, were they? When you complained to him, 'These terms are worse than anything offered to us before,' I'm told he answered, 'Well, of course they bloody well are! You've turned down everything since the talks on Tiger *and* Fearless, *and ever since the 1960s!'*[6]

Yes, I think that was the sort of 'theme'. I don't vouch for those exact words. But basically the situation was that they were trying to get me out of the scene, because up to this particular date, at Lancaster House, I had always got the better of them. Their tactic, obviously, was to remove Smith and then deal with people who were less

6 Anglo-Rhodesian negotiations were held aboard HMS *Tiger* and between Prime Minister Harold Wilson and Ian Smith in November–December 1966; a subsequent series of talks was held aboard HMS *Fearless* in Gibraltar in 1968.

experienced, and less capable, than Smith. They succeeded in doing that. Thereafter, they succeeded in selling their agreement to people who were inexperienced and naïve. People have said to me, subsequently, that they wished they had listened to me, and 'how right' I was. But, I repeat, they had fallen among the sharks of the underground political world. I've said before, 'diplomacy' is a word for which the British Foreign Office is famous. I think the word was *coined* by the Foreign Office. To me, British 'diplomacy' is a polite word for deceit. In other words, whenever you come to an agreement with anybody, or talk to them, you do it in such a manner that it can subsequently be interpreted in at least two different ways, preferably *three* different ways – so that you can never be cornered. *That* is British diplomacy.

Did you expect the Patriotic Front to agree to the terms of the Lancaster House conference?

I thought they would, because I saw it would be advantageous to them. My interpretation, as I told them all at Lancaster House, was that this was going to give us a Patriotic Front government. Obviously, under those circumstances, they would regard it as a victory.

Yet there seems to have been a fairly widely held view that the Patriotic Front might walk out in the end?

Yes, because I think they wanted more. But, I had no doubt in *my* mind, knowing them, and what their tactics would be, that we would land up, as a result of Lancaster House, with a Patriotic Front government. I was accused of being alarmist. I was very depressed. Certainly, I could not get rid of my belief that it *would* mean a Patriotic Front government and that that was going to be disastrous for my country. So I was not in a very helpful frame of mind.

Subsequently the head of your Rhodesian Intelligence service, Ken Flower, has published his diaries and says that Lancaster House 'knocked the stuffing out of us'.[7] *Did it knock the stuffing out of you?*

I wouldn't use that expression because I had been through so many experiences and disappointments. This was just another one. Maybe it was the *coup de grâce*, but I had learned to ride these things. I did not just sit down and give up hope. I hoped that my predictions would prove wrong.

Ian Smith saw only Rhodesia. The flexibility of the British ministers and

7 Ken Flower, *Serving Secretly* (London, John Murray, 1987), p. 249.

Foreign Office officials, men of so many missions and abortive attempts to propel him towards a settlement, are all part of his demonology. The 'topspin' which Ian Smith manages to impart to the word diplomacy needs to be heard, the better to convey his derision. One met with something of the same acerbity, I remember, in a jurist of distinction, who had 'stayed on' in one of Britain's former African colonies. Reflecting on officials of the Foreign and Commonwealth Office he met out from London, during the frequent comings and goings in the sixties when de-colonization was accelerating, he said, 'They all seemed to be called "Julian" or "Adrian" and they all seemed to say "How are we going to play *this* one, Julian?" or "Adrian"?' Such detachment, and what was taken to be implicit acceptance of historical inevitability, roused sentiments which differed little from Ian Smith's opinion of 'diplomacy'. This jurist was another who had found the long history of mass de-colonization and the accompanying constitutional changes implemented in country after country, on a franchise of 'one man one vote', in no way encouraging.

The aversion Ian Smith continues to nurture, particularly for Conservatives, like the late Lord Butler, and Lord Carrington, was warmly reciprocated. Lord Carrington loads Ian Smith with a personal responsibility for fifteen years of lost opportunities, and blames him for 'the whole thing'. But what ruling class has ever given up its position voluntarily if it knew that its power would dissolve if it did?

'If I may add in passing,' **Ian Smith** was fond of saying, and delivered himself as follows.

> Our biggest problems, and the most devious behaviour, as far as British politicians are concerned, we found to be among Conservatives – who were supposed to be our friends. Not among people like Harold Wilson, who many people thought was my greatest enemy. No so. I found him honest and straightforward in my dealings with him. It was people like Rab Butler and Carrington who were the ones who deceived us, and misled us, and who went back on undertakings that they had given us.

At Lancaster House, the problem for British diplomacy was not the demands of those who, like the Patriotic Front, *sought* power. One could always decide to give in to that. The same question arises in relation to the IRA, or the PLO. The problem for the diplomat was to persuade those who *held* power to *yield* it. Lord Carrington's first endeavours, Mr Smith agrees, were to winnow him out. **Lord Carrington** himself baulked at the suggestion of any crude intention to move Ian Smith aside.

Ian Smith moved *himself* aside. I think he started off, and probably ended, by not wanting a settlement or an agreement. But, there were people around him who *did* want it. I think he was greatly pushed aside by his own people and finally he left the Lancaster House conference – certainly a long time before it ended. That, I think, made things a good deal easier. But I, or we the British, did not 'move him aside'. It was his own people.

Ian Smith reports you as saying, when he challenged you that Lancaster House was going to lead to a Patriotic Front government, 'But my dear Mr Smith, the whole thing has been designed to see that that does not *happen.'*

I don't know why I should have said that. The whole thing was designed to get a settlement with majority rule. But Mr Smith proved a little bit difficult, of course, on occasions, and we did not perhaps exactly see eye to eye.

But is that an exchange that you recall yourself?

No. What we were working for, and genuinely working for, was a settlement which brought about majority rule and to enable the people of Rhodesia to decide who they wanted. What would have been most agreeable to the British government at the time, would *not* have been the Patriotic Front. There is no point in pretending otherwise. Obviously, most people at that time would have preferred the Muzorewa government to go along. But, there was no suggestion of it being *rigged* so that the Muzorewa government should continue.

However, had the possibility of the final outcome, a Patriotic Front government, been acknowledged by you, Lancaster House would never have taken place. You would never have got Smith to go there.

No, of course not.

What about Mrs Thatcher? Was her acceptance of a constitutional conference and the pursuit of a constitutional settlement based, would you say, on the slight risk or the probability that it would bring Mugabe to power?

I think about half-way between those. I think that there was always the possibility it would bring the Patriotic Front to power. At the *beginning* of the conference it was thought to be less likely than it clearly was at the end of the conference.

Ian Smith did not attend the constitutional conference at Lancaster House riddled with curiosity about its possibilities. Of the delegates assembled, he had one thing only in common with Robert Mugabe. He did not want agreement. Mr Mugabe felt like that, because he was convinced he was going to win the war in the end, and in war winners take all. Mr Smith felt like that, because he feared the total eclipse of European rule then represented in Bishop Muzorewa's multi-racial government. Ian Smith's suspicion was that Lancaster House was a Trojan horse for the Patriotic Front, and seldom had wood been put to such unwise purposes since that time. At Lancaster House, Mr Smith tried to bar progress on points which the British could not concede. Poor hand though **Ian Smith** had by this time, how had he determined to try and play it?

> If I may put it bluntly and crudely, I tried to influence the people with whom I was working in the transitional government, that they were being taken for a ride by the British government. I remember telling Carrington, at Lancaster House, that this agreement he was trying to sell us *would* land us with a Patriotic Front government and, in other words, a pro-communist government. That's why I was accused of being an 'alarmist' which was, of course, the story put about in the corridors of Lancaster House.
>
> *What did Carrington say, when you told him that what he was doing would 'land us with a Patriotic Front government'?*
>
> He said to me 'My dear Mr Smith' – I remember it so clearly – 'My dear Mr Smith,' he said, 'I want to assure you that the whole thing has been designed to ensure the very opposite.' He said, 'We are satisfied that, under this agreement which we are now selling you, there will be a government of national unity with Bishop Muzorewa, Nkomo and Smith.' I told him that, from my experience, I just could not see this and I wanted to alert him to the fact that we would land up with a Patriotic Front government. I repeat, I was then accused of being an alarmist. History, clearly, has proved me correct and Carrington, and the rest of them, wrong. This is another excellent example of how people in Britain, and especially British politicians, think they know more about my country than *I* do, and not only my country, everybody else's country with whom they are dealing. They were wrong.

It will be noted that, as recounted by Ian Smith, who 'remembers it so clearly', Lord Carrington spoke of his satisfaction that there would likely be a government of national unity of Bishop Muzorewa, Nkomo and Smith. In other words, he did not include Mr Mugabe. There was a belief, early on, that the Patriotic Front might not hold together, and that while Nkomo would likely stay in, Mugabe would walk out. Lord Carrington has acknowledged that while he considered Lancaster House might bring the Patriotic Front to power, 'At the beginning of the conference it was thought to be less likely than it clearly was at the end of the conference.' To Ian Smith's plaintive sense of grievance was allied an almost Calvinist conviction, as strong as that of John Knox himself, that he alone could be right.

The egalitarian pretence of Westminster democracy in Africa – where the safeguards of a freely elected parliament, an independent judiciary, a Bill of Rights and the protection of the rule of law all too often had become a screen behind which one-party dictatorships felt at liberty to impose their own tyrannies – was something which a determined hierarchy like Ian Smith's was incapable of accepting. He made a last ditch stand against it at Lancaster House. Yet, as Lord Carrington has said, 'he was gradually being pushed aside by his own people'. One link in this chain forged behind the scenes was Air Vice-Marshal Harold Hawkins, the commander of the Rhodesian Air Force at the time of UDI, who had been head of the Rhodesian diplomatic mission in South Africa, and who was Bishop Muzorewa's foreign affairs adviser on the delegation at Lancaster House. It was the Rhodesian military who told Ian Smith, in the end, that the war was unwinnable and that he should draw appropriate conclusions. Ian Smith's claim that he saw, at the outset, that Lancaster House would 'land Rhodesia with a Patriotic Front, pro-communist government', according to **Air Vice-Marshal Harold Hawkins**, is a case of looking in the rear view mirror. Unlike Mr Smith, Hawkins *did* see a last opportunity at Lancaster House.

Since the nationalist parties had been left out of the Muzorewa 'election', if we may call it that, I felt that we were going to have a tough time making that one stick anyway, with or without British recognition. Therefore, personally, I welcomed the chance for another round of negotiations under Britain's auspices and particularly as they were to be held in London.

What did you assume was the underlying British objective at Lancaster House?

I thought it was to get a just settlement. I felt that the evidence of the Muzorewa election would have to be taken into account, and that in any subsequent election that might emerge, the Bishop – who had led the hybrid of Zimbabwe–Rhodesia for those few months – had as good a chance of winning as anybody else.

Ian Smith says that he saw through the Lancaster House process very early on. He says that he challenged Carrington that Lancaster House would inevitably, he thought, return a Patriotic Front government. To which Lord

Carrington replied, according to Ian Smith, 'But, my dear Mr Smith, the whole thing has been designed to ensure the very opposite. 'Is that your recollection?

I was not privy to that exchange. But no, I do not think that what Mr Smith thought is what we *all* thought. Not at all. As far as Mr Smith having seen what the aim was with 'great clarity', as he claims, well then I wish he had told *us* about it a bit earlier. He did not do so. In fact, he would always be suspicious of the British government. That was a stand he was very consistent in throughout all the various periods of negotiation over the years. We missed a golden opportunity at the time of HMS *Fearless* in 1968. On those terms, the then army commander and I went along to Ian Smith, the Prime Minister, with an appreciation of the threat drawn up, and the likely course of events if we rejected the *Fearless* proposals. Bear in mind that, at that time, there were no sanctions, and there was no terrorist war. We urged him to accept the settlement terms. We said to him that we knew there were some elements on the right of his Cabinet who would wish to turn them down, but that our advice to him was to accept. We got a good hearing from him but he did not accept the *Fearless* terms. I always thought that was a great, a very, very great mistake.

Flower, the head of the CIO, the Rhodesian Intelligence organization, seems to suggest that Smith had a mole in his character which meant that, despite his public personality as a man of single-minded purpose, it was rather his weakness to be unable to make up his mind. He couldn't bring himself to say yes?

I think so. I do not think there was ever much flexibility in Mr Smith's mind. I could understand that, to a degree. But he had a rather limited vision of events in the wider field. He was totally negative, all the time, in his approach to the Lancaster House conference.

The South Africans acted in support of a constitutional outcome at Lancaster House, although their Foreign Minister, Pik Botha, had expressed concern to Lord Carrington that because it was taking so long there to achieve one, Bishop Muzorewa's electoral prospects were receding. Time was on the side of the Patriotic Front, improving their military and now their political position.

Lord Carrington, who was the hinge on which all doors turned at Lancaster House, had closed a door firmly on Ian Smith soon after the conference began. In doing so he had a 'confidential ally' in the South Africans.

They were in favour of a settlement, of course. In favour of a settlement which would have an outcome of which they approved, obviously goes without saying. But, they wanted a settlement and really, on the whole, they were fairly helpful about it. They wanted a settlement because they were spending a very, very large sum of money. There were quite a lot of South Africans involved in Rhodesia, and so from their point of view, a settlement was a good thing. They were encouraging it.

How did you counter the argument that the South African Foreign Secretary, Pik Botha, was to use when he said that every week spent in Lancaster House meant the Bishop was losing 5 per cent of the vote? That the possibility of achieving a moderate government was eroding all the time, and the longer the conference went on?

I do not think that really made much sense, to be truthful. Pik Botha, in point of fact, was quite helpful during the Lancaster House conference. The South African government were just as anxious for a settlement which was acceptable to everybody as the front-line states, and the British, were. The South Africans did not prove at all obstinate, or recalcitrant, in anything they did. Everybody wanted a settlement, if they could get it. Of course they wanted their *own* settlement. They wanted the result to be convenient to them. Certainly, at Lancaster House, the South Africans proved to be quite helpful in the background.

For the first time in all the years he had confronted British governments, at Lancaster House Ian Smith was not, as he was so concerned to point out, 'in sole control'. We have his word for it that, had he been, he would not have attended at all. However, the eclipse of the embattled Smith was one of the evolving coincidences which led to the final agreement. By then, and for the first time since his illegal declaration of independence in 1965, Ian Smith had wanted something from Britain. It was something only Britain could give. Recognition of his internal settlement. Only then might confidence return, and with it the necessary support for continuing, if needs be, the war. Without this recognition, the illegal independence which Smith had so long ago declared, and which Bishop Muzorewa believed was his own rightful due as the new Prime Minister, would stand exposed as fictional. In the sequel to Henry Kissinger's initiative with the South African Prime Minister, John Vorster, in 1975, Ian Smith had been forced into a corner during his crucial meeting with Kissinger in Pretoria on 19 September 1976. Five days later, as a result of the South African arm-twisting he has described earlier, Smith had literally stood on his head in conceding the principle of black majority rule. That which he had once vowed would never come in a thousand years, would now arrive in two.

Whereupon, Bishop Muzorewa had been elected Prime Minister of a predominantly black administration in Rhodesia. Blaming the British, as he does, for most things that have befallen him and white Rhodesians, how many of the objectives of this 'internal settlement' did **Ian Smith**, himself, consider had been met by the time of the Lusaka and Lancaster House conferences in the autumn of 1979?

In this country, all of them. The six principles that were laid down by the Conservatives and then, subsequently, by Harold Wilson had all been complied with.

But, there was no end to the fighting, and there was worldwide non-recognition of your internal settlement, including non-recognition by South Africa.

I don't think that is strictly correct because South Africa was never in a position where they did not recognize us. You say there was no recognition from the world, well of course there *couldn't* be until Britain had recognized us. That was the key to the whole thing. We only wanted recognition from Britain. The fighting continued simply because Britain would not recognize us. We were satisfied that the moment we were recognized by Britain the fighting would end. As long as Britain did not recognize us, she was virtually siding with the terrorist movement.

However, the call by Muzorewa for the Patriotic Front forces to surrender had met with little or no response. Fighting was intensifying.

That is true, because these people were concerned. The more concerned they were, the more they decided to intensify the fighting, because they thought they might lose out. So, obviously, their intentions were to try to prove to Britain, and to the rest of the world, that they were not going to go along with this agreement.[8] How *could* they accept it? It would have meant that they had lost! The only way they would have accepted it would have been if Britain had acknowledged us, and then that would have been the end.

Rather difficult to see how it would have meant 'the end'. You would still have been left with guerrilla forces, in very substantial numbers, in the sanctuary areas of the neighbouring states, Mozambique and Zambia.

8 I.e. Smith's settlement with the 'internal' black leadership and the Muzorewa government.

Yeah, but if they knew that Britain was no longer opposed to us, and that Britain was going to support *us*, we could only have been strengthened. If Britain had supported us it would have meant the end of sanctions. This was our biggest problem, always. Sanctions and *economic* war. It would have reinstated confidence within our country. You see the biggest blow to us was *after* that agreement with Vorster and Kissinger. From that moment on, we started losing Rhodesians. People who had previously been prepared to go along with it said, if we have now got to accept a philosophy which is going to put us in the same position as these countries around us which, as we can see, simply leads to chaos and confusion and bankruptcy, then we know there is no future. So from that moment on we started to bleed. We started to lose our skills, our professionalism, our know-how, our investment. Recognition from Britain would have changed that.

Ian Smith was trapped. He turned, in the end, to the Britain he renounced at the time of UDI for the salvation he had sought, but not found, in South Africa. The adoption by the South African Prime Minister, John Vorster, of a policy of 'détente' towards the black states to Pretoria's north in the mid-1970s was an attempt to achieve a regional settlement. It called for a constellation of moderate black governments, including eventual majority rule in Rhodesia. Vorster at first had not been able to exact more from Smith than the release of some nationalist leaders in detention in Rhodesia, including Sithole and Mugabe. The latter, having no interest in détente, had made his way to Mozambique to organize the ZANU insurgency. Smith had done all he could to frustrate this South African policy. Indeed, he had undermined Vorster's strategy, holding out against its implementation and refusing to allow Rhodesia, as he has said earlier, 'to be used as a sacrificial lamb in helping to solve South Africa's problem'. The South African Foreign Minister, **Pik Botha**, makes it clear that Pretoria did not forgive Ian Smith for that.

Mr Vorster tried, at a relatively early stage, in the mid-1970s, to point out to Mr Smith what we termed, at that time, 'the alternatives'. We felt he should have accepted the proposals made then. We had felt it our duty to point out to him all along what he could do, and what he could not do, in terms of his capabilities, military, economic and financial. We could never be seen to *prescribe* to Mr Smith. Any such attempt would have had dire political consequences inside South Africa. But we had to be honest with him and pointed out the limitations imposed by all these various factors and say there was only so much we could do, and no more, and that it was up to him to decide what would be the best course for his government.

I myself was very intimately and directly concerned, both as Minister for Foreign Affairs and, before that, when I was ambassador in Washington. I arranged for Dr Henry Kissinger to meet with Mr Vorster in Germany in 1976 and later, as you know, Henry Kissinger came to South Africa. We did not *force* Mr Smith. It would be correct to say that we could not meet the demands, or requests, Mr Smith made to carry on the war. That is a different matter from suggesting we cut the ground from underneath him.

What was South Africa's contribution to the settlement of the long, vexatious dispute over Rhodesia?

Looking back, I think the role we played to get people like Mr Sithole released showed a very clear intention on the part of the South African government to contribute towards a peaceful solution in that country. It is an important country to our north. You know as well as I do that you cannot have peace in South Africa if all the states surrounding us are continuously engaged in internal conflict. It affects our economy in the long run. Secondly, there was the role Mr Vorster played in South African government in being honest with Mr Smith. He said to him often, 'Look, *you* must make the judgement, but you must make it in terms of *realities.* Of what you can do, and cannot do.'

There were at that stage, I think, twenty-four black Rhodesians for every white Rhodesian. That order of figures, those numbers, were against any idea of perpetuating a white-controlled government in those circumstances.

Would it be right to see that as the controlling fact in your minds determining policy here, in South Africa, that the ratio of black and white in Rhodesia was so much higher than your own?

It was certainly one element. The country had never achieved independence. Britain persistently claimed sovereignty. It was therefore not for the South African government to attempt to influence Rhodesia to follow either our policies, or our line of constitutional development. We steadfastly held to the principle that it was a British-cum-Rhodesian affair. Our task was to point out to Mr Smith his alternatives in terms of his capacities, and at the point it became clear to us that it was all getting too difficult. The war was spreading. He could not get the war under control, and eventually it was affecting *our* security interests.

For all its high and healthy open spaces, Rhodesia is so hemmed in that perhaps the mind was accordingly narrowed. Ian Smith was always dismissive of how his fixed policies might come to be viewed by others. His attempt to persuade South Africa to incorporate Rhodesia's destiny with its own could not carry the earthworks of Afrikaaner thought and dogma. Buried in Pik Botha's answer is the importance played in any such consideration by what the Afrikaaners saw as white Rhodesia's hopeless arithmetic. Twenty-four blacks to every white in Rhodesia. Five to one in South Africa. The logic of Ian Smith's Rhodesian future had been an Anglo-Saxon and Afrikaaner ascendency over the black. History suggests that opportunity passed as long ago perhaps as Queen Victoria's century, with Dr Jameson's raid, and Cecil Rhodes's attempt to bring down Kruger and the independent republic of the Afrikaaners. Will historians be right to suggest that **Ian Smith**'s miscalculation of South African responses was rooted in the integrity of that old enmity?

I don't believe that is an accurate interpretation. From my previous contacts with the South African leaders, even before John Vorster became Prime Minister, I was given to understand very clearly that as far as they were concerned they were pragmatic about the whole of southern Africa, and the need to work with us in order to preserve the white civilization that had been established in southern Africa. I remember John Vorster saying to me that there was no doubt, in his mind, that the Zambesi should be the dividing line, and a much more realistic dividing line, to try to draw in Africa. We were both conscious of the fact that the main threat was Russian imperialist aggression in Africa. That was the very first briefing I recall that I had, from my security chiefs, when I took the chair as Prime Minister. So, we had a common enemy there, which was communism, and which was on the march down Africa. I think that was far more important to the South Africans than thinking about what had taken place at the beginning of the century. Although they might have had many differences of opinion with the British, I think they certainly preferred them infinitely to the Russians.

Perhaps so, but not at all costs when it came to their view of themselves and their own interests. After all, Vorster chose detention in South Africa for some years, during the Second World War, rather than joining the cause for which Britain, supported by Rhodesia, joined – the fight against Hitler.

Yes. But, I would say this to you. At least we had one thing in common – we had *defied* Britain. We were both on the same side as far as that was concerned. In the last war we fought the Germans, but we've forgotten about that, haven't we? We are now working with them, because we realize that there are greater evils on this earth.

Marxism–Leninism and Russia. So I think I can honestly say to you that I don't believe that was a factor. We were both in the same boat in that we were both fighting against the British, one can put it that way.

The wars South Africa has intermittently waged or supported across its frontiers are not acquisitive, its Foreign Minister maintains, and therefore are to be distinguished from the imperialism and colonialism of the British. The ox wagons of Afrikaaner nationalism stopped at the Limpopo. The bandwagon of apartheid was halted there as an act of South African policy, and not on the Zambesi which Ian Smith, and he maintains John Vorster also, considered to be 'the much more realistic dividing line in southern Africa'. But, according to **Pik Botha**, all that was made clear to Ian Smith at the time of Ian Smith's Declaration of Independence.

We were not consulted on that declaration at all. I do not know what we would have advised him. My inclination would have been to tell him 'No, don't do it.' But, that is history. Naturally, you can imagine, there was strong sympathy in this country with the Rhodesian government's feelings because we saw that the same attempts that were being made to isolate Mr Smith, and force him into submission, eventually would one day be made in respect of the Republic of South Africa.

How do you think history should see this particular question? Where, and why, does the idea of an Anglo-Saxon and Afrikaaner paramountcy in all of southern Africa come to grief? Was 1923 the parting of the ways? Did it, as some people might suppose, come to grief almost at once with Dr Jameson's raid and Rhodes's attempt to bring down Kruger's republic?

Yes, there was the referendum in the twenties in Rhodesia, on whether they wanted to join the then Union of South Africa or remain, as they were at that time, a colony. Later on they naturally received more autonomy from Britain. Yes, they did not want to join us at that time. That is quite correct. But, even before UDI was declared, the relationship between Rhodesia and South Africa was very good. Because a large number of Afrikaaners, and Afrikaans-speaking persons, emigrated to Rhodesia and were living there. It was a substantial number.

But all the time Smith is trying to get you to agree that it is your interests, as much as his, which dictate some kind of Anglo-Saxon–Afrikaaner paramountcy as far north as the Zambesi River. The frontier as you *see it is the Limpopo. Why does he fail in these efforts?*

Because, in the first instance, you will find that in South Africa, we just do not have a record of being an empire. We have never claimed, we have never gone beyond our borders to take. We have always regarded Britain as the colonial power. We were taken, and defeated. So you will find a natural inhibition, on the part of the Afrikaaner, to engage in extra-territorial military activities, in order to *conquer*. The South West Africa case is one case in point. There was a rebellion inside South Africa among the whites, when General Louis Botha, the first Prime Minister of the Union, invaded what was then called German South West Africa. A large section of the Afrikaaner actually came into open rebellion against General Louis Botha, because he did that. So you have that historical antecedent which I think is part of our make-up. Take another case in point. Lesotho, Botswana, Swaziland, the old former so-called High Commission territories, which were then Bechuanaland, Swaziland and Basutoland. In terms of the Union Act of 1910 it was at least envisaged that they could one day join South Africa in terms of a plebiscite or referendum. Dr Verwoerd unilaterally waived that possibility, and abandoned it completely.

South Africa's conclusion that white rule beyond its own frontiers could not be maintained left Ian Smith stranded. Following the urgency of Macmillan's 'wind of change' speech in 1960, the prevailing British sentiment of censorious moral rectitude over Rhodesia, contrasted with its *realpolitik* towards South Africa, might lend itself to not wholly unmerited charges of hypocrisy. Invited to search his memory for instances where Britain admittedly did right concerning the issue of Rhodesia, Ian Smith declares them to be rare. The white paramountcy in Rhodesia ended as it had begun. Lobengula, King of the Matabele, had risen against Cecil Rhodes and company rule in the 1890s, and Ian Smith could not withstand the black rebellion which triumphed in 1980.

I would remind you that Rhodes made an agreement with Lobengula before there was any rebellion. So he tried to do it the right way. It was only when the Matabele went against it that there was a rebellion, but to begin with it was a peaceful agreement. This happened with most of British and French colonialism. It was only after the last world war that the scene changed. The communists decided that they wanted to get the free world out, so they said colonialism was a bad thing. Regrettably, foolishly, the free world accepted this and allowed themselves to be branded as exploiters. I think that is the tragedy, because they did a wonderful thing in developing this part of the world.

One has the feeling that you scarcely suspected that, beneath the surface of colonial life in Africa, there was all the time festering a black nationalism of such intensity?

I would say to you that black nationalism was *not* of such intensity. This I can assure you – and many people would support what I say – that we had the happiest race relations in this country that you would have found anywhere in the African continent. I could not get over the number of times, when I was Prime Minister, that I met people, and bumped into people, who said to me the thing which strikes us more than anything else are the happy black faces we see in this country. Happier than anywhere else in this world. There were a few disgruntled politicians who wanted to be the government 'tomorrow' but, you know, all politicians who are not 'government' tend to become disgruntled. All they had to do was to comply with the constitution and, in time, they would have got there. But, they were not prepared to do that. So they went and set themselves up outside because they could not get what they wanted constitutionally. They came to the conclusion it would take them too long and decided that they were going to act unconstitutionally. They could not, even then, get support from the internal blacks, until they started resorting to terrorism. I would remind you that most of the terrorism that took place in this country was against the black people. Not against the white people. Eventually it did come against the whites, but its main objective was to intimidate blacks into supporting them. Blacks who, otherwise, would not have supported them.

What verdict would you accept of yourself in all this? Let me put you in elevated company. Lord Milner,[9] one of the great figures of empire, said of Rhodes that 'he was undaunted by former failure and untaught by it.' Is there something in that of you?

I will leave that to you and to others to decide. I believe history will sit in judgement on me and maybe it's premature at this stage to try to do this. We honestly and genuinely tried to do what we believed was right. We had a constitution in which there was no racial discrimination. It was just a meritocracy, and we honestly believed

9 Governor of Cape Colony 1897–1901, member of Lloyd George's War Cabinet and Secretary for War 1918–19. His concept of the empire was that of a permanent and organic union, not an alliance of self-governing colonies.

that in the end this would produce the best government for our country. A government composed of black and white, but of people who had been educated into the democratic system of government. I have always said that I believe the metropolitan powers were wrong when they pulled out of Africa and then said to the governments they left behind, 'We will only give you independence when you have installed the Westminster democratic system of government.' They said this to people who did not believe in the Westminster democratic system, and who had never practised it themselves. And what does history show? That it has failed. Everywhere where they have implanted it, it is not working. It has not succeeded. I say to people – and they are surprised to hear my answer – 'Do you know how many times governments in Africa, to the north of us, have changed hands through the ballot box?' Never. It is one of the sadnesses of this world, I believe, that the British and other people have allowed the communists to brainwash them into believing that colonialism was a bad thing.

And for you it was a great achievement.

For anybody with any intelligence and sense it *was* a great achievement. To spread the light of Western Christian civilization surely is a wonderful thing, when one looks at how these people advanced and developed here after colonialism. The proof is there. But the communists wanted the metropolitan powers of the free world out so that they could come in, and of course communist propaganda is very effective.

Take the achievement of a place like Salisbury, which is an achievement. Seventy, eighty, ninety years ago it was 'a dirty stream in a marshy land' as someone has said.

Just bush.

Today, it's a city with boulevards and thoroughfares. What verdict on it all is justified? It begins with Cecil Rhodes, and with rebellion very quickly by the Matabele and Mashona. Why was the final outcome not the same?

I think that was the way it *would* have gone had the rest of the world not interfered and particularly allowed the communists to interfere. Look at the irony of the situation where we are today. In the end the solution was imposed by Britain, one of the leading countries of the free world. As I told them at Lancaster House it would, it ended up by the installation of a Marxist–Leninist communist government here. That is how successful the British have been in the free world. Isn't it sad?

Like some Cincinnatus of the West, in the 1960s Ian Douglas Smith assumed the role of the yeoman farmer of antique virtue and simple manners called from the plough to preserve his Rome, surrounded and in danger of defeat and with it the retreat of Western civilization.

With the end of empire and at the level of statecraft the British had long since accepted, there could be no more escape for them into the world of Rider Haggard, King Solomon's Mines and Alan Quartermaine. More reluctantly, they also became persuaded that it was an unreal world which Ian Smith inhabited. What he stood for was against the grain of British political thinking. Or rather, it could not be made a matter of practical politics.

Lancaster House was the melancholy twilight of white rule in Rhodesia. Sunset for Ian Smith himself. The climax was now approaching. Lord Carrington prepared to shoot the rapids with the Patriotic Front.

5
Carrington Shoots the Rapids

The Lancaster House conference dragged on interminably through the autumn of 1979. Long before the end it had become a wearing ordeal but, so long as it held together, it remained the off-chance of a lifetime to get a Rhodesian settlement. Unlike Lord Rosebery, Prime Minister at the time Britain was pegging out her colonial claims in Africa and of whom Churchill had said, 'In a wearing ordeal, his thoughts strayed to the fine speech he could make on resignation,'[1] the combination of Lord Carrington and Margaret Thatcher continued to drive the conference on, step by step. The most difficult issue of all had been left until last. It was to bring about a cease-fire in a civil war which had cost twenty thousand lives and made a million homeless. Even when, and if, achieved, any cease-fire was bound to be fragile, and the pre-election period extremely tense.

The British were determined not to permit additions to, or subtractions from, the agreement reached by the Commonwealth heads of government when they met in Lusaka, which had entrusted Britain with proposing the basis of a settlement to the warring parties, and then supervising new elections in which all parties could take part. Lord Carrington's price for assuming these obligations was his right to exclude 'outsiders'.

Neither a role for the United Nations, nor one for the Organization of African Unity, was acceptable to the Smith and Muzorewa parties in Rhodesia. The Commonwealth had already largely played its part, at Lusaka, and included among the 'extraneous influences' that Lord Carrington now wished to keep at arm's length was Sir Shridath Ramphal, the Secretary General of the Commonwealth. Carrington's tactics required finesse, for if the heats and ferments of the Rhodesian issue were to be kept 'within the family' and out of the international

1 Winston Churchill, 'The Earl of Rosebery', in *Great Contemporaries* (London, Collins, 1937), p. 20.

arena, Britain needed international acquiescence at all stages of its strategy.

After exhaustive discussions with the rival delegations at Lancaster House, Muzorewa's 'Salisbury' delegation, and the Patriotic Front, Lord Carrington had laid before them, on 3 October 1979, a full description of the new constitution for Rhodesia which he intended to propose to Parliament in Westminster. The Patriotic Front and the Salisbury delegation could not come to any agreement between themselves, and so it fell to Britain to set out and make clear what they, the British, believed must be the basis of a constitutional settlement. Now, said Lord Carrington, he needed to know, in order for the conference to proceed any further, whether both delegations accepted this constitution. Both Mr Mugabe and Mr Nkomo said the Patriotic Front could not agree to the constitution until the transitional arrangements had been discussed. Conforming to his step by step approach, Lord Carrington had replied that the constitution must be decided first. However, agreement on the constitution could be made contingent on agreement on the arrangements to be made during the period of transition to independence, a time which would be both highly flammable and saturated with mutual suspicions.

Up to this point, the Salisbury delegation's position was that the only purpose of the conference at Lancaster House was to decide the constitution. But the key to international acceptance of the outcome was a fresh general election and Carrington made clear the British commitment to it being held. This had been the crucial element, contained in the Lusaka agreement, in relation to the pre-independence arrangements.

On 15 October Bishop Muzorewa announced that his delegation accepted elections which would be supervised under the authority of the British government. Whereupon, on 19 October, the Patriotic Front announced for their part that, if they were satisfied about the transitional arrangements, 'they would not have to revert to discussion of the constitution'. Lord Carrington's 'spider tactics', as Mr Nkomo called them, meant the conference was thus able to go on to the next stage, and against the background of agreement on the independence constitution.

A new constitution having been agreed, and with Ian Smith isolated and Bishop Muzorewa agreeing to stand aside and yield his executive authority as Prime Minister during fresh elections, the struggle for power in Rhodesia was nearing its climax. Excitement mounted, suspicion heightened, as the final reckoning drew near. Although Britain sought the widest possible international recognition for a settlement, this was not a condition. Lord Carrington has acknowledged the British preference for a Muzorewa, or Muzorewa–Nkomo, government. As he said, all concerned had their prejudices.

So, also, did the Secretary General of the Commonwealth, Sir 'Sonny' Ramphal. Ramphal proved a vigilant gadfly for Lord Carrington. He had organized what amounted to a parallel conference in London while that at Lancaster House was in session. There were no less than thirty-two meetings of Commonwealth High Commissioners held in London in order to exert pressure. Denied any direct influence inside Lancaster House, **Sir Shridath 'Sonny' Ramphal** was not to be caught with nothing to say, and he made determined inroads on Lord Carrington's freedom of action.

I saw my role, and the Commonwealth Secretariat's role, as holding the British government to Lusaka, which was hammered out. It wasn't easy or something very workable, but it was going to require sticking to Lusaka. If that began to unravel we would lose it all. I recognized that the British government would be under great pressure from many quarters, from the Conservative Party itself, from South Africa, from Ian Smith and his colleagues in Rhodesia and, possibly, from British public opinion. But that was not the whole story. I knew that the front-line states themselves, Africa and the OAU, would be under a great deal of pressure from the Patriotic Front. Joshua Nkomo's first remark to me after we had concluded the Lusaka conference was, 'Who gave authority to the Commonwealth to settle the future for us?' It was a valid question.

What did you reply?

I said, 'We have not settled it for you. We have given *you* a chance to get it settled.' We had put them in a corner really. We'd made it necessary for them to talk. We'd made them sit down at the table in Lancaster House. For our part, it was terribly important that, having used that kind of pressure tactic on the Patriotic Front, we in the Commonwealth should see that the deal which had brought them there was faithfully respected. We had a responsibility as we saw it. The meetings of the Commonwealth High Commissioners during the Lancaster House conference were designed not to thwart the British government, but to ensure that the British government got it right. Also, that the Patriotic Front got it right. I spent many nights with Nkomo and Mugabe in their London apartments talking them into postures of agreement.

But there is something in your attitude which does not accord with Britain's behaviour in other years. The British had divested themselves of colonies, your own included,[2] *on a consistent basis over all the years since the Second World War. You appear to have had a heightened suspicion that this process may have been about to be reversed in some way?*

I think we should be clear what that suspicion was. There was never any thought, in anyone's mind, that the processes of the election as carried out, or put in place, by the British government would not be fair and that it would not be a Westminster-type of election. But there were wide areas of transition to election, and the electoral process itself, that lent themselves to distortion. This was not for reasons that were 'Machiavellian', but for reasons which had to do with the politics of the situation on the ground. For example, the exclusion of Mugabe's party on the grounds of intimidation. As was very seriously threatened.

How did the 'disqualification issue' present itself to you?

The disqualification issue arose *there*, at that point. There were issues that the Commonwealth observer team had to deal with on the ground, in relation to the election commission, and they were there as a confidence-building mechanism. It was terribly important to the Patriotic Front, that they should have been there. The Patriotic Front were very suspicious. Surely, with good reason. They were coming out of the bush. They were giving up arms. They were putting it all on the table. They were dealing with a British government which they knew, four or five months before, in its election manifesto, had gone for a Muzorewa government. They were taking this all on trust. I think rightly. But it meant something to them to have the back-up of the Commonwealth there.

But, in consequence of Lusaka, the British had emerged with their minimum objective intact. Free elections were to be held under British, *not United Nations, OAU, or any other kind of supervision. A British governor was to be installed in Salisbury during the transitional period with full colonial powers and freedom to act. As Secretary General of the Commonwealth, what had you thought of that?*

I thought the outcome was good but I recognized that there were some 'grey' areas left. Deliberately so. Yes, the British had stated their case that they were in charge of elections and they did not want a United Nations presence. But the Patriotic Front had *not* given up the idea of an international presence. What was agreed, in the Lusaka accord, was that there were to be free and fair elections, properly supervised, on the British government's authority with Commonwealth

2 Formerly British Guiana, now Guyana.

'observers'. Now, that left the question of proper supervision for further discussion. Bear in mind that this was an agreement reached between governments, between the front-line states and the British government. But the Patriotic Front and the Rhodesian government, who were the real contenders at Lancaster House, were of course not parties to it. The concept of Commonwealth observers was fully written into the Lusaka agreement. As I saw it, these elements were left for further negotiation.

If I may repeat to you the relevant words of that agreement at Lusaka, although you have quoted them accurately, it says, 'The government formed must be chosen through free and fair elections, properly supervised, under British government authority and with *Commonwealth observers.' It does not mention any* authority *as belonging to those observers. It seems clear enough that 'authority' lies with the British government; however, that was the argument you had with Carrington?*

The ultimate authority rested with the British government. They were resuming constitutional authority. Soames would have the executive and legislative power,[3] and they would run the elections, but they would have to give *meaning* to the role of Commonwealth observers. They would have to give it meaning, not just because it was written down in black and white, but for very good reasons. What was going to be important was that, once this government was elected it won recognition. It could have been, from the point of view of the British government, *any* government. Indeed, there were many reasons to suggest that for a long time Lord Carrington thought it would be a Muzorewa government, or a Muzorewa–Nkomo government. But, whatever emerged needed the stamp of legitimacy. The Commonwealth observer team would ultimately provide that, by its certificate of the election. That is why it was a very important concept. The British, I think, became very nervous of any kind of interference. They objected to me, they objected to the Commonwealth, they objected even more strenuously to the United Nations and the OAU. They had, in the end, to settle for a full-blooded, straight-up, Commonwealth observer mission.

When, in late November, the British were told that there had got *to be a Commonwealth observer group, it was at a meeting of the Southern Africa committee. How was it that Britain, as you put it, 'had to settle' for a full-blooded role for a Commonwealth mission?*

3 Lord Soames flew out to Rhodesia on 12 December 1979 to prepare for, hold and supervise elections leading to full independence.

It was all coming to a head. This was the unresolved, unspoken issue which had to be faced. Peter Carrington's approach to it was, 'OK, we agreed that there should be Commonwealth observers.' Or rather, as you said, '*with*' Commonwealth observers. He said, 'We are going to invite all Commonwealth countries to do what they like in relation to sending observers.' So any Commonwealth country could send observers and thus, we would end up with Commonwealth observers.

In saying that, he also meant that the British were still to be the sole judges of what was 'free and fair'.

He meant that, but he also meant that there should be no 'collective' – that is the point – no collective Commonwealth observer group, that would make a *collective* 'Commonwealth' pronouncement. I must not use the word 'devious', but it had other implications. Inviting Commonwealth countries to send observers really meant leaving it to the few countries who could afford it – that is, the richer Commonwealth countries on their own. It meant, in effect, that you would not have had anything like Commonwealth observers *across the board.* It meant too that you would not have had a *single* report. You might have had a *multiplicity* of reports. One group might say it was 'free and fair', another might say it was not, and then you could take your pick. Now, that would never have sufficed. The difference between Lord Carrington and myself was that *I* saw the Commonwealth presence as being a collective presence, reporting ultimately to the Commonwealth heads of government. I am glad to say that we prevailed. I am glad to say we prevailed, in *his* own interests, and in the interests of the British government.

But would you agree that all this arose out of your personal determination not to see Mugabe defeated in sight of the Promised Land?

Not to see the Patriotic Front *as such* defeated. We were not making choices between Mugabe and Nkomo. Many of us felt very sure that there was a groundswell of opinion in Rhodesia that would install a Patriotic Front government.

How did you interpret those British objections at the time, what did you suspect underlay them?

I think they worked on the basis that the fewer extraneous elements in this situation, the better. I did not think there was a Machiavellian move to rig the election, let nobody say it. I did not think that for one moment. But, I thought that they were anxious, as indeed they were, right through the Lancaster House negotiations, to have a completely free hand. I recognized, and I think most of the Commonwealth recognized, that in the end, that was not even in the interest of the British government. Of course, as it turned out, the thing that really *was* very much in their interest was that the Commonwealth team did pronounce the elections to be 'free and fair'.

It would not be right, therefore, to suggest that you thought that at this stage the British were working to exclude the Patriotic Front, Mugabe in particular, if possible, and their concern was – to use a theatrical metaphor – that if you 'got into the act', that might not prove to be possible?

No. I did not think they had such a settled plan, but that they would have a notion that there could be many 'contingencies', that 'we may have to do many things, and we do not know what they may be,' and therefore to have Commonwealth people 'in the way, and probably pronouncing against us', then really, 'that was not going to be in our interests at all.'

Do you recognize this as Lord Carrington's position? That he believed, whatever the Commonwealth governments might have thought that they had agreed at Lusaka, that a Commonwealth observer presence of the kind that you *wanted could undermine the flexibility of Soames, the Governor, as he tried to juggle with the very great complexities of elections in a nominal cease-fire that might break down altogether?*

Yes. Well, of course, it was the juggling that we were concerned with. And you see that juggling could have been pretty important. There was a stage, remember, in the run-up to the final agreement at Lancaster House, when the Foreign Office began talking about the 'second-class option'. The second-class option was an agreement at Lancaster House, *without* the Patriotic Front. Now, this is explained away, *ex post facto*, as applying pressure. I think it would be wrong to dismiss it. It could have become quite serious. The Commonwealth took a very strong line, and Commonwealth High Commissioners in London intervened on that issue. They made it clear that Lusaka had agreed on a formula based on the consent of *all* the parties, and that there was no way that the Commonwealth was going to stand by and see a Lancaster House formula which excluded the Patriotic Front. So, when you take that further down the road into the elections, you realize that there could be a situation in which there would be distortions in the arrangements. In fact, that actually arose. There was talk of 'intimidation'. There was the suggestion that perhaps small parts of the country could be excluded from the election. Again, the Commonwealth observers had a good deal to say in relation to that and I think they headed off any such arrangement which really would have been devastating.

Statesmen do not have much time. The exertions of Sir 'Sonny' Ramphal made for delay when Carrington wanted, above all, to reach a final accord quickly. Patriotic Front guerrillas were being infiltrated all the time into Rhodesia to begin campaigning, a test of nerve for the internal parties which nearly unravelled the conference.

But giving reassurance at Lancaster House was like applying embrocation to an elephant. There was not enough to go round. Still, notwithstanding all the rancour and reproaches, Lord Carrington massaged his way on.

By now the leader of the ZANU party, Robert Mugabe, was almost day by day enhancing the formidable impression he had made on all minds at Lancaster House. In consequence, the heat haze above the conference table was beginning to clear, and the outcome in Rhodesia which the British ministers and officials had once considered to be the least desirable was now more clearly on the cards.

Sir Michael Palliser, who had served in Africa and on several visits had accompanied the then Prime Minister, Harold Wilson, as private secretary, was now the head of the Foreign Office and the diplomatic service.

The dominance of Mugabe, or the force of personality of Mugabe, was something that emerged at the conference itself, rather than before the conference. By that I mean the military situation was known, but the importance of the figure himself I think was not really appreciated until he turned up in London for Lancaster House.

Would it be true to say that the quality of Mugabe's performance at Lancaster House influenced the Foreign Office advisers and their advice? That here was somebody whom we may have hoped to exclude from power but with whom, as a result of seeing him in action at Lancaster House, we realized we might have to deal in the end anyway?

Yes, I think that is true. We knew Joshua Nkomo. Nkomo had been around for a long time, of course. He had been imprisoned by Smith's regime for a long time but previous Prime Ministers had visited him. Harold Wilson went and saw him and spoke to him. So, Nkomo was a quite well known figure. Muzorewa had *become* a fairly well known figure, not so much in personal terms as in what people had seen of him in Salisbury. Mugabe was, in that sense, more of an unknown. Therefore, perhaps, he made more of an impact. I think as a person, Mugabe made a very powerful impact. It was not, at all times, a wholly favourable one. Mugabe could be very unpleasant.

In what respect?

Oh, in the way that he conducted himself in negotations, and spoke, and discussed. He had a very sharp, sometimes rather aggressive, and unpleasant manner. Nkomo is a sort of African volcano, and is a much more traditional African figure – one which I think British colonial figures, and others, were more accustomed to dealing with. Mugabe was rather a new type of animal.

In what way was he a new type?

As I say, he was sharper. He was more direct. He did not 'blow up' in smoke like Nkomo. He got rather acid, and rather unpleasant. He clearly had a considerable intellectual power. I do not say Nkomo hasn't. With Nkomo you had the sense – I'm speaking now very personally – of the wily African chief who uses his great size, and his great girth, and his capacity to blow his top, all of it very carefully calculated. It was something that you see in any African gathering of the elders. That is the way they run things. This is not to say that he was not intelligent. I think he *is* intelligent – and wily. *But*, I think his intellect is not as sharp as Mugabe's. Mugabe was a more Westernized figure. Whether that owes something to his education in a Catholic seminary[4] I do not know but, certainly, his intellectual approach is much more like that of a Western-educated man than that of Nkomo.

Robert Mugabe dazzled at Lancaster House. But those who dazzle arouse suspicion in eyes trained to shine less brightly. The Foreign Office, and the ministers they advised, had to make a judgement whether Mr Mugabe was to be regarded as a figure familiar to a generation of British officials who had become accustomed to dealing with African nationalists. Was he to be seen as one of Professor Harold Laski's children?[5] Or, more disturbingly, was he one of Lenin's?

While this was a matter for close and continuing argument, one is conscious always of the ruling impulse of British policy, the need to cut the Gordian knot of Rhodesia. That need was strongly felt by Lord Carrington's number two, as Foreign Office Minister of State, Sir Ian Gilmour. With Carrington in the Lords, Gilmour spoke for Britain's foreign policy in the House of Commons. He was a participant in the negotiations throughout Lancaster House, in addition to which, as Lord Privy Seal, **Sir Ian Gilmour** also had a seat in Mrs Thatcher's Cabinet.

4 Mr Mugabe received his early education from the Jesuits at Kutama mission school near Salisbury.

5 Professor Harold Laski was Professor of Political Science at the London School of Economics from 1926 and taught a modified Marxism. He died in 1950 and had a considerable influence on African nationalists.

Mr Mugabe took a more ideological line than Mr Nkomo, throughout the negotiations. Because there was more suspicion of him, anyway, I think that those suspicions remained throughout most of the conference. People thought that he was much more 'hard-line' than Joshua was. To some extent, at that stage, he was.

What were your personal impressions of him?

Extremely intelligent, and a very good debater. One of the problems was, as I think Ian Smith complained, that the Patriotic Front walked all over the other side! Because Bishop Muzorewa, who was a charming man, found great difficulty in opening his mouth in debate, and found it very difficult to say anything at all cogent. Mr Sithole was clever, but really not taking any great part. So I think that when Mr Smith complained, in a perhaps unfortunate phrase, about 'his blacks not being anything like as good as the other blacks', he was absolutely right. Ideologically, or at least as far as debating went, the Patriotic Front were vastly superior to the other side.

Was that important enough in your mind, and in Lord Carrington's, for you to draw the appropriate conclusion from it?

Not particularly. Although the prospect of Mr Mugabe winning the election was clearly there, it was not as inevitable then, or did not seem as inevitable then, as it now seems. It was generally thought that the Bishop would do better than he did. And, of course, it was by no means certain that Joshua Nkomo and Robert Mugabe would stick together. There was always the chance that the Patriotic Front would split up and that you might get a combination of Muzorewa and parts of Nkomo, or the whole of Nkomo. It did not look as though it could be a cut and dried result, at that time, at Lancaster House.

Was that the gamble that you were making? That Mugabe would not *win a majority, and that therefore the British would be able to manipulate some coalition at the end bringing in, for example, Nkomo, to reinforce the internal settlement?*

It was not the gamble that I was making. Obviously, there may have been different views. It certainly was thought that Joshua might move around a bit. But, to me, and I think to others also, it still seemed that the right thing to do was *to get a settlement.* Even if that meant the Patriotic Front winning. Firstly, because it was the only way of ending the civil war in Rhodesia. Secondly, and less important, but nevertheless quite important in itself, it was the only way of getting the Rhodesian canker out of British politics.

Therefore, when Lord Carrington talked, as he quite often did, and as the Prime Minister did, of the option of a 'second class solution', to be avoided if possible, but to be adopted if necessary, how real a prospect ever was the 'second class' solution?

The second class solution being a deal with Bishop Muzorewa? Well, if the Lancaster House conference had failed, and after all it only just succeeded – and there were several moments when it was very very near failure indeed – if it had failed then, however undesirable it would have been, and I think it would have been very undesirable for the interests of this country, it would have been extremely difficult to avoid the second class solution. It would have created a great deal of trouble for us, but it would have been difficult to avoid. But, to my mind, it was always extremely undesirable. It might well have happened.

What was your personal attitude to the 'second class' option?

I was wholly against it.

Some people in a position to know recall your saying, at one stage, in a discussion with officials present, 'You must be mad even to think of it, let alone suggest it.'

Who, me? Yes, I'm sure. I would not dispute that.

In other words, there was one single objective you were pursuing at Lancaster House. It was to be rid of the Rhodesia commitment?

Yes.

The possibility, as Sir Ian Gilmour put it, that 'Joshua might move around a bit', was not the least of the differences, tribal and political, that separated Joshua Nkomo from Robert Mugabe. It was a split that never really healed and it divided the nationalist movement between the advocates of non-violence and those who, much earlier, had convinced themselves of the need for revolution and armed 'struggle'. The personal rivalry between the two for leadership reached back as far as 1960. Nkomo's willingness to entertain proposals for a Rhodesian settlement on a restricted African franchise which had been made by Duncan Sandys, then colonial secretary, marked the parting of the ways for **Robert Mugabe**.

That was the reason we finally broke away in 1963 and formed ZANU. We felt we could be more dynamic with a new leader and with younger people, and I was one of those younger leaders. I believed that we had to be more militant, and that Nkomo appeared to be compromising all the time and to be afraid of launching the party as a new *fighting* force with more and sharper teeth than a mere political and non-violent party.

The future President of Zimbabwe, as Lord Carrington said, was someone he had tried hard to meet before becoming Foreign Secretary in Margaret Thatcher's government. Mugabe had refused to do so. He had remained relatively unknown to the British. Lancaster House therefore afforded a protracted opportunity to form a judgement of his qualities and what he stood for. Mr Mugabe talked in Marxist categories and aroused suspicion because of that. Sir Ian Gilmour considered him to be 'more ideological ... and much more hard-line than Joshua'. Among the things predicted, which it may be presumed Britain wished to avert, was the extension of communist influence in an area of importance to Britain and the West. Soviet policy was to keep pots boiling in southern Africa. Britain's Foreign Secretary was exercising responsibility without the correlative of real power, and spheres of influence are not replaceable, or removable, by moralizing about them. Lancaster House itself represented a compromise between the opposed positions of Britain on the one hand and the Patriotic Front of Nkomo's ZAPU and Mugabe's ZANU parties on the other. The personal conclusions **Lord Carrington** reached about the Patriotic Front leaders, and in particular the nature of Robert Mugabe's political ambition, must be seen as of critical importance.

It was quite obvious that there were differences between the ZAPU and ZANU, but they were, nominally, a coalition and, nominally, speaking together. We thought of them more as nationalistic, than as representatives of either China or of the Soviet Union. Quite clearly, what the Soviet Union was doing was to use Nkomo to try and increase their influence in southern Africa. To some extent it backfired on them because of the fact that Mr Nkomo's army did not really do much fighting. It was Mr Mugabe's army that was really doing all the fighting.

Incidentally, what interpretation did you place on that? Was Nkomo getting ready to fight Mugabe?

That was one interpretation, certainly. Whether it was the right one I do not know, but certainly there was a very large Nkomo army in, and around, Lusaka and in Zambia generally, which of course was extremely unpalatable to President Kaunda. It was much larger than *his* army, and it was being armed by the Russians. This is one of the reasons why President Kaunda was very anxious to get a settlement, because he had all these armed soldiers in his country who were not all that well disciplined.

Therefore, if your broad policy imperative was to exclude Soviet influence where possible in southern Africa, then because of that, Mr Mugabe's coming to power, the man without *Soviet patronage, actually helps to secure that interest?*

Yes. I do not think that anybody seriously thought that Mr Nkomo was under Soviet influence very much. After all, he was known to a great many people. I don't think he seemed to be a very likely tool for the Soviet Union.

President Machel of Mozambique had urged the British to accept that Mugabe and his followers 'were not communists, as we are communists'. Were you persuaded by that?

I don't think Mr Mugabe ever suggested he was anything other than a Marxist. But he also made it fairly plain that his Marxism was compounded of a good deal of common sense, as well as ideology. One of the reasons for that was that he had been exiled for a great number of years, and he saw what happened, not just in Mozambique, but also in Tanzania, when very left-wing policies were pursued and the economy was dictated by Marxist ideology. He saw what had happened, particularly in Mozambique, when all the Portuguese in effect were removed. I thought that he was, and that he *is*, determined not to be the Prime Minister of a country which is bankrupt; and bankrupt really as a result of ideology, rather than of good sense.

An important source of knowledge for these judgements was the reporting from Mozambique, the host country to Robert Mugabe's forces in the sanctuaries it provided just inside its long frontier running north and east around Rhodesia. The Foreign Office identified Mozambique early as offering an opportunity to gain some leverage over events and also Mugabe's ambitions. It proceeded to conduct a remarkably successful diplomacy following which the President of Mozambique, Samora Machel, delivered more perhaps than Lord Carrington could have hoped. At the time of Lancaster House, an officer of confidence, whose varied and sometimes esoteric career in the foreign service, from Cyprus to El Salvador to Cuba, gave him a feel for the 'revolutionary' culture, was sent to Maputo, formerly Lourenço Marques, Mozambique's capital. This was the British ambassador to Mozambique, **Achilles Papadopoulos**.

My brief was unmistakable. It was that what was going on at Lancaster House, which had started before I left London, was very important indeed, that the position of Mozambique would be crucial, and that we had an important and delicate task to perform, in Maputo, in carrying Mozambique along the path of discussion, negotiation, reconciliation and solution. So, the importance of Mozambique was never underestimated.

What indications were given to you of Machel's interest in achieving a settlement of the Rhodesian issue?

Machel himself gave very clear indications indeed. At the presentation of credentials ceremony – which, as you know, is usually one confined to innocuous expressions of goodwill – after the usual pleasantries were over, Machel immediately had a bottle of champagne opened and he said 'Now, Mr Ambassador, we have work to do!' We got down to it there and then. It was quite clear, from that first conversation, that he thought that the time had come for a settlement. He was very anxious to help in any way to promote a just and equitable solution, and he looked forward to us working together towards that end. That was, from the word go. Once persuaded, as both Machel and Chissano were, that what we were proposing was fair and just, they undertook immediately to use their best endeavours with Mugabe. Of all the front-line states, Machel's Mozambique was, of course, suffering the most. Remember that the Portuguese had left. Although it was not Portuguese government policy, when they went it was almost a scorched earth, 'everything must collapse after us' attitude. Portuguese who left Mozambique in droves fearing for their lives, and for their property, left behind nothing. They left Mozambique in a very weakened state indeed. The new Mozambiquans, from Machel downwards, were a bunch of young, keen, energetic and patriotic people who had great visions of the future they were going to build. They were an interesting mixture of 100 per cent Africans, some white Portuguese, a few Asians of mostly Goanese extraction, and some 'in-betweens'. They were all professing to work for a Marxist–Leninist solution to their problems. I doubt if very many of them were as well read in their Marxist theory and philosophy as they claimed to be. Of course, none of them had had any experience of government, with the result that they had big problems, with a capital 'B' and a capital 'P'. In addition to which they had to deal with a national resistance movement inside Mozambique, now called 'Renamo'. Machel's support for Mugabe's struggle in Zimbabwe had made all these problems worse still.

So from what considerations do you think Machel's decisive pressure on Mugabe arose?

Primarily, the parlous state of Mozambique and its economy. He wanted to address these problems effectively and he knew that he could not do it while there was a war going on next door, and while he still had these commitments to the Patriotic Front. In addition to which, he was always in danger of attack because of his support for the war against Smith.

Presumably, it was part of your brief as ambassador to urge upon Machel that he 'must act now' otherwise he stood to lose everything?

Shall we say that there was a confluence of interest, at that time. HMG had decided that the time had come to resolve the long-standing question of Rhodesia, and Mozambique – Machel in particular – had decided that the time was right and that, above all, he could trust the British government to do right. We were both aiming at the same thing.

What was the relationship between Mugabe and Machel?

There was no doubt that Mugabe was very conscious that his position of strength owed much to the support that Machel had given him – a base for his operations in Mozambique, and a border across which he could come and go more or less as he pleased. Also, and I did not realize the extent of this myself until after the elections, to the degree of support given to Mugabe by FRELIMO units inside Rhodesia. Later, we were asked to arrange for the repatriation of several hundred FRELIMO fighters who had been infiltrated into Rhodesia. Machel regarded Mugabe as a freedom-fighter, fighting an iniquitous system, and he owed it as one freedom-fighter to another to help in any way he could.

The British, of course, were called upon to make, at various stages, a very important judgement about Mugabe and whose interests a victory for him would secure. For your part, what view did you form of Mugabe?

He struck me as a very serious-minded man who knew where he was going, and who knew that time was on his side. He had rattled those in Rhodesia, like Smith and his government, who believed that eventually they could put this thing down. Mugabe had shown that it was an extremely difficult, if not impossible, thing to put down, and he knew it. So much so, that he could afford to turn down offers of help, so it was said, for example from the Eastern European bloc. Rumour had it that while the Soviet bloc would be ready to help

Mugabe, there would be strings attached. These were, mainly, that Mugabe should support the Soviet Union in all sorts of international fora over the problems they were having with the Chinese. Now, the Chinese were helping *Mugabe* at that time. Partly because of that, but I believe mainly also on principle, Mugabe would not have any strings attached. So there was this, I don't know if you would call it 'animosity', but this 'stand-off' over such offers.

You were in place in Mozambique as Lancaster House unfolded. How was Machel endeavouring to influence the outcome there?

He was, of course, kept informed on a daily basis. Not only by us, but by his man there, Fernando Honwana, who later, sadly, was on Machel's plane and died with him. Machel was also in close touch with the other front-line statesmen. I always had the impression that, although he would not 'break ranks', as it were, when the other front-line statesmen made a collective *démarche* on whatever they feared we might be doing, or not doing, Machel took care always to be constructive and avoid the more extreme language of some of his colleagues.

I remember, after Lancaster House, when we were leading up to the election and the front-line statesmen issued a very strongly worded statement against our tactics, I was summoned by Machel to be given his version of their *démarche*, and I sensed that he still trusted us. He did not go overboard in the way that some of the more emotional front-line statesmen did.

What assurances was he seeking?

It could all be summed up in one sentence really. It was that we should allow a free expression of opinion by the people of Zimbabwe and he would abide by whatever that decision was.

So, after it was all over, after Lancaster House and after Mugabe's victory, what do you recall of your meetings with Machel?

They were very easy, very friendly, and at times exuberant. He never missed an opportunity to sing the praises of Margaret Thatcher. The impression he gave, if I may say so, was that 'there was a woman he could do business with!'[6] Indeed, he said so openly. It was at a gathering of all ambassadors on 3 or 4 January 1980. We were all summoned to the Presidential palace, in Maputo. This was an annual

6 Mrs Thatcher's frequently quoted response to her first meeting with Mr Gorbachev, that he was 'a man she could do business with', had become common currency at the time of this interview.

thing, and Machel made a little speech, a kind of state of the nation, a state of the continent, impromptu speech. Most of it was, obviously, devoted to Lancaster House and the achievement of the conference. He would seek me out and he would raise his glass for everybody to see, and say for everybody to hear, 'I think, Ambassador, we have done well, do you not think so? I think a toast to Margaret Thatcher is in order, don't you?' And I said, 'But *of course*, Mr President!' (laughter) I could not help watching the expression on the face of a certain ambassador during this exchange!

A British success was a Russian reversal. It was given to the British ambassador, Achilles Papadopoulos, to observe the discomfort with which his Soviet counterpart was made acquainted with Pliny's ancient dictum '*ex Africa semper aliquid novi*' – 'out of Africa, always something new'.

The limitations of victory have been written on many a soiled landscape. The young self-proclaimed Marxist revolutionaries of FRELIMO, like Samora Machel and Joaquim Chissano, who had won power in 1975, had found such limitations writ very large in Mozambique. Now, nearing their climax, the Lancaster House discussions were taking place against a background of heavy Rhodesian raids. 'Behold the abomination of desolation', said the prophet Daniel, and desolation, both economic and military, was indeed the prospect before Mozambique. It was primarily out of this consideration, as Ambassador Papadopoulos said, that the probably decisive pressure which Machel brought to bear on Robert Mugabe arose. Machel's Foreign Minister at the time, now the President of Mozambique following Machel's death, was **Joaquim Chissano**. President Chissano confirms the blunt terms in which, following their meeting in Havana, just before Lancaster House, Machel had told Mr Mugabe of Mozambique's expectations of the London conference, and what he must expect from his hosts in Mozambique if he chose to go on with the guerrilla war rather than continue to pursue the constitutional opportunity at Lancaster House.

We were sure that if the Patriotic Front behaved in the way we felt that it *should* behave, when we talked to them in Havana, the results of Lancaster House would be positive.

When deadlock was reached, in November, two months or more into the conference, when Lord Carrington was poised with a 'yes or no' ultimatum to the Patriotic Front, Mr Mugabe appeared ready to break at that moment and walk out of the conference. What attitude did you take with Mugabe over that?

We advised him not to break. Because, our consensus in the front-line states was that by no means should we break these talks. Neither the liberation movements should despair, nor the front-line states should advise any kind of break. If any break came at Lancaster House it should come from Smith and Muzorewa, or maybe from the British, but never from the liberation movement or the front-line states.

There were particularly important exchanges between President Machel and Mr Mugabe over this point. The diplomats, both in the Foreign Office and other foreign services, are fairly consistent in their version of what happened. It is said that President Machel said to Mr Mugabe 'If you do walk out, you can have a villa in Maputo', a life in exile, but that was all.

It is true. I don't myself remember the exact wording. There were piles of paper on this. But the essence of the message was – and Machel had said it also in Havana – that we, in Mozambique, had consented to so many sacrifices, but, we would not consent to *more* sacrifices for a cause which could be won by this conference and a chance which might be spoiled by the liberation movement. It is true that President Machel was very firm that we should not lose the chances that were offered to us at Lancaster House and that therefore we would not consent to any further and unnecessary sacrifices. We had closed our border and consented to all this economic devastation of our country. We knew that we were winning, militarily, against Ian Smith. They were losing so many planes here, near our border, and they were about to have their southern routes closed by FRELIMO forces participating in Zimbabwe. So, we knew the situation and we knew the strength of the Patriotic Front, particularly the strength of ZANU. We were not afraid of the outcome. We felt it was time to stop, and start developing our country.

Why then was Mr Mugabe so concerned that he doubted your optimism?

Maybe he knew the British better than we did. The Patriotic Front were afraid they would be outmanoeuvred; and especially over how their forces, and the Smith and Muzorewa forces, could co-exist. What did the British have in mind? But to us it was clear that Britain had decided that Ian Smith was no longer a man to be considered either a friend or in the interests of Britain. Not any more.

But, whereas the Patriotic Front had seen the Lusaka Accord reached by the Commonwealth heads of government and the all-party conference at Lancaster House as a calculated diminishment of the role and status of the Patriotic

Front, Mozambique, which had won a 'liberation war' itself, does not take that view. Mozambique trusts the British.

Yes, we did trust the British. We continue to do so today.

Each successive step at Lancaster House proved more difficult than the last. Lord Carrington had hoped that with the new constitution, and provision for fresh elections agreed, a cease-fire would quickly follow. However, it was to take more than another month to settle terms under which the guerrilla forces would return to designated assembly points inside Rhodesia, without, as they saw it, the risk of destruction there so serious that they could not fight again. Carrington had already declared it infeasible to integrate the armed forces of the opposing sides, or to make any other such radical changes before the elections themselves were held. Once again, and because the opposing sides could not begin to agree themselves, he had put forward a British outline proposal for this pre-independence period. There would be a British Governor, Lord Soames, who would have all executive and legislative authority. All the political leaders would be required to commit themselves to the election campaign. With this proposal on the table at Lancaster House, the military temperature in Rhodesia and on its borders was rising steadily. On whether, or at which point precisely, a determination by **Robert Mugabe** to quit the Lancaster House conference was deflected by President Machel's insistence, Mr Mugabe's own recollections are more guarded. Was he preparing to walk out at the time of Lord Carrington's final proposals over the assembly areas for Patriotic Front troops inside Rhodesia?

Yes. We actually said no for a start, and then Lord Carrington conceded and they worked out an assembly point in the heartland of the country. Thereafter, he said there would be nothing more. This was as far as they could go. But, at that stage we had said we wanted another.

The diplomats relate the story that you were in fact determined to break on this issue and only Machel restrained you.

No, we defied Machel on that one completely. Machel would have wanted us to accept even *before* the first concession was made! On that one we said, 'No. In the ultimate it is our own salvation, and we will not go.' If Honwana were alive he would tell you. I said 'No' to him. We said 'No' to Sonny Ramphal and to everyone else. Our soldiers could have been decimated by a well organized attack in the positions which they had been given.

Can we just clarify these crucial exchanges between you and Machel, your host in those sanctuaries in Mozambique when all this begins. He urges you, persuades you, at Lusaka, to go to Lancaster House, which you attend under protest. The story is that he told you point blank when you did not wish to go, or wished to break at Lancaster House that, if you did, all you would be granted was 'a villa in Maputo'.

No, he never said so. Not to me. It never came to me that way, never.

Did that represent his thinking, as you understood it, as to the choice that you faced?

No, I don't think Machel went that far. If somebody said that, or was given that to say to me, then he didn't bring it to me like that.

But whereas Nkomo, and ZAPU, were to tell you that they would not go back to Zambia, and not only because their host Kaunda would not welcome them there, are you saying that you could have gone back and continued the war from Machel's Mozambique?

Yes, we could have gone back and continued the war; but we also knew, of course, that the Mozambiquans had grown weary of the war. They wanted settlement. They wanted an opportunity to devote their energies to the welfare of their own people. We were quite sure that we could continue the war, even with minimum support, because we had created within the country definite areas which were liberated. There could have been a fight from within the country.

The Cubans had urged such a course upon Robert Mugabe during the Havana meeting of the non-aligned nations held on 7–9 September 1979, immediately preceding Lancaster House.

Joshua Nkomo took another view of the realities at this stage. While he says it was touch and go whether the Patriotic Front walked out of Lancaster House, he is less equivocal about the role played finally by Machel and the constraints of Machel's advice on Mugabe, be it in Havana or in the course of the London conference.

I suppose you have to start really with Havana, and then go to the conference itself, but Machel was constant in saying of the constitutional approach, 'Whatever it is, take it!' Take it and work your way forward then from *within* Zimbabwe.' He was very determined. And pretty tough with Robert.

Which meant that Mugabe was either making an empty threat of walking out and continuing the war, or that he was going to defy Machel?

Defy Machel, and go where?

'Defy Machel – and go where?' described a matter of fact concerning Robert Mugabe and ZANU's freedom of action which secured a vital flank for Lord Carrington's diplomacy. The Foreign Secretary also had a flank to guard at home. Carrington still had to face his own side. He had to bind the party to him. The issue of continuing sanctions against Rhodesia remained alive, of course, and was still as divisive as any in British politics. While the Lancaster House conference was sitting, the British government was fast approaching a date, 15 November, by which sections of the Rhodesia Act of 1965, under which various sanctions orders had been made, fell due for renewal. The determination to allow these sanctions to lapse as soon as practically possible had been foreshadowed in the party's manifesto for the 1979 general election. The Conservative Party conference of 1979, held in Blackpool following Mrs Thatcher's victory, took place during the crucial stages of Lancaster House. **Julian Amery** led the last stand of the Conservative right for British recognition of the achievement of Ian Smith's internal settlement – and against Lord Carrington.

> The year before, at the Brighton conference, the platform had refused to call me, and there was quite a demonstration in the hall of people who thought I *ought* to have been called. Come the debate in 1979, I do not think that Lord Carrington won the argument. I think what dominated the conference was that the Conservative government had just won the election. It was a triumphal conference, and Peter was a very popular figure in the party, quite rightly; although I think that, left to themselves, probably a majority of delegates would have shared my view if it had been put by the platform. If the platform had said 'we're going to recognize, and we are going to lift the sanctions', I think they would have had overwhelming majority of the conference on their side. But the conference was not minded to issue a major rebuff to the new government, and to a popular Foreign Secretary.

None the less, there was no mistaking the import of the ovation which Amery, the government's arch-critic over Rhodesia, won at Blackpool. There had been a nip of 'Munich' in the air. Lord Carrington knew only too well that if he was unlucky in his appeasements, what had been applauded as virtuous endeavour at Lancaster House would quickly be condemned, 'if it all went wrong', as abject trimming.

The corollary of the British cultivation of Mozambique's decisive influence in helping to nudge Mugabe towards a constitutional settlement, and bring about an end to the insurgency was that the chance of the result Britain would have preferred in Rhodesia, which might be described in the beginning as 'anybody but Mugabe', was sensibly diminished. In Lord Carrington's masterly speech to his party's conference, he had said, 'I do not know what the outcome of the [Lancaster House] conference will be.' He also included this: 'There are some I know who wish to move ahead regardless of the risk of bringing about a collapse of the Lancaster House conference. To them I would say this: think what a *settlement* would mean for the lives and welfare of all the Rhodesian people. Think what it would mean if we throw over the chance of a settlement at this stage. Equally, to others, I say this: No one will be allowed to decide, unilaterally, that Rhodesia must continue in illegality, war and isolation.'[7]

The speech was construed as benefiting Bishop Muzorewa's administration by seeking to build on it, by gaining international recognition for it and if possible inducing the Patriotic Front to join the constitutional process and lay down its arms, and that this was the object of the government's complex diplomacy. It was a speech to which **Lord Carrington** says he gave more careful thought than almost any he had made.

> I got a standing ovation too! You forgot to say that – and I won the debate by a very large and overwhelming majority. So, perhaps Julian [Amery] was satisfied with his standing ovation.
>
> *How divided was the party, at this stage, over what you were doing?*
>
> Well there was certainly a body of right-wing Conservatives who felt very strongly that this was the wrong thing to do. They were perfectly entitled to that point of view but they have never, in my judgement, answered the criticisms, or the problems that I think would have arisen if we had not gone along the course we did. I think they were wrong, and I think they have been proved to be wrong.

Lord Carrington's winning over of the party faithful at Blackpool suggested that although white Rhodesia's future excited sizeable sympathy, as time had worn on compassion was dwindling. As Cecil Rhodes had done in his time, Ian Smith had relied for the protection and consolidation of his position on a group of active parliamentary supporters in England. Amery believed, and encouraged the belief, that Carrington was not *bound* to accept an outcome at Lancaster House, which could be considered against the British and Rhodesian interest. To the end, **Julian Amery** ran a determined interference against Carrington's projected settlement.

7 Conservative Central Office, 10 October 1979.

I think the last initiative I took was to try to help break up the Lancaster House conference. It was something that only the delegation[8] could do itself. I urged them to break it up, and I urged Bishop Muzorewa to go back to Rhodesia as Prime Minister.

To break it up on what grounds?

That he did not like what he was being asked to agree to. Notably, and among other things, he was asked to step down from the Premiership which, in a community like Rhodesia where prestige is rather important, meant that he was no longer a dominant figure.

From Amery's viewpoint, the Lancaster House conference was deplorably timed. Parliament was not sitting and *The Times*, whose letters page has been called 'the jungle drums of the British establishment' was no longer being published because of its protracted industrial strike. Amery's drumming, over what might be taking shape at Lancaster House, stirred up apathy while, at the same time, Westminster had its mind on inaction.

Everybody was away. You could reach them, or reach some of the public through the television and the newspapers, but it was not a good season for mobilizing parliamentary support. There was no House of Commons sitting, and there was not going to be. By the time the House of Commons met at the end of October, the vital stages at Lancaster House were more or less finished. There were still possibilities of breaking up the conference, but this would have depended on Muzorewa and Mr Smith. Mr Smith wanted to do that. But Muzorewa and a number of the senior Rhodesians, white as well as black, were – what shall I say – 'nobbled' by the skill of the Foreign Office. Even the Royal Family were brought into play.

In what respect?

It was how some of the senior military figures, the white 'establishment', were fêted rather, and taken to see the Queen Mother. Things of that sort. The Queen Mother was known to be a great friend of Rhodesia. They were taken aside afterwards and told, you know, 'We don't want to break your friendship with the British establishment.' It was a game that I had seen played with Sir Roy Welensky in an earlier phase.

Julian Amery's reference is pointed. Rhodesia's ubiquitous ghosts were looking on. Sir Roy Welenksy, the principal architect of the Federation

8 I.e. the Salisbury delegation of Muzorewa and Smith.

of the Rhodesias[9] in the 1950s, had seen his creation fall in ruins because, it seemed to him, the successors of the British imperial heritage in London had lost their nerve and become indifferent – that heavily charged word for conservatives – 'appeasers'.

By December 1979, the situation in and around Rhodesia had reached a critical stage. The struggle for military, and with it of course political, advantage intensified. Each side was claiming to control 90 per cent of the population. If the negotiations in London were not brought rapidly to an end, the probability was increasing of a total breakdown. The time had come for Nkomo and Mugabe, of the Patriotic Front, to take their last and hardest decisions: whether to agree that their forces should assemble inside Rhodesia and to commit their futures to elections on the basis of a return to colonial rule under a British Governor. There had been several occasions when the conference had seemed likely to break down. Mr Mugabe suggests that his mind was changed in the end not so much by the fact that there was now considerable international support for Lord Carrington's final proposals as by incurable factional differences within the Patriotic Front – the differences between himself and Mr Nkomo over whether to fight on. The wrangle over the number, and location, of assembly points was the ultimate issue for **Robert Mugabe**; they held the key to influence over the vote in the coming election.

> We stood our ground, because now it had to do with the fighters, it had to do with the very instrument we had used to create the favourable situation that existed in 1979. In that situation you had Smith and Muzorewa showing a willingness to negotiate, to give up UDI, and to accept majority rule. If we were weak on this point, we would find our soldiers placed in positions which would reduce them from the strong instrument we had built and developed to a much weaker instrument. They would have given up most of their arms and they would have been in assembly areas which gave a greater advantage to the Rhodesian forces than to us. We insisted that they should keep their arms, at least for their own protection. Then came the question, where would they be placed? It was in working these points out that we faced great problems.
>
> *Then the British made a crucial concession. That was the stationing of British and Commonwealth forces in the assembly areas,* with *the Patriotic Front troops, which precluded the possibility of any attack on them that was not also an attack on the British army.*

9 The Central African Federation – see note 21 to chapter 1.

Yes. We welcomed that because it was the really vital element and it prevented the Rhodesian forces, you see, supported by the South African forces – who were in the country, don't forget – from attacking our assembly points. There were nasty incidents here and there. Yes, that was really vital.

None the less, this was the issue on which you were prepared to break and walk out of the conference at the expiry of Lord Carrington's 'yes or no' ultimatum during the drawn-out arguments over the cease-fire proposals?

Yes. At that stage, and before we conceded to Carrington, our partners of ZAPU came to us and said, 'Comrades, we want to give you the ZAPU position clearly. We do not intend', Nkomo said to me, 'to go back to Zambia, whatever happens.' Which meant acceptance of the situation, you see, whatever happened.

It meant that Nkomo would make an agreement.

That is right. The message was clear.

What did you say?

I said, 'Oh I see. That's *it*, is it?' Then, on the ZANU side, we met alone. We had persisted in our adamant position for some time, but when this came we said, 'Fine. Let's accept.'

'Let's accept' were the words from Robert Mugabe which, in effect, were to end Rhodesia's civil war.

On 7 December, in an effort to force the pace at Lancaster House, the British announced Lord Soames's appointment as Governor. He went to Salisbury on 12 December, before the cease-fire had been finally agreed. The Governor's arrival was intended to deprive all concerned of any incentive to delay or prevaricate further at the conference table.

At midday on 21 December 1979, in a ceremony at Lancaster House, the final agreements were signed. The conference had lasted more than three months. Even so, there was no certainty about anything in the future. It had always been plain that even if an agreement could be reached at Lancaster House, the difficulties of implementing it would be no less formidable.

6

One Vote, One Man!

Until the very last days of the Lancaster House conference, in December 1979, Lord Carrington had been privately despondent about its chances of success. With the opposing sides 'fighting to negotiate', the bush war continued and the habit of killing had made rapid advance.

Carrington's gifts of charm and ease as a diplomat have won a general salute, but he also had the gift of confining them. He had run the meetings at Lancaster House in a manner variously described as 'autocratic' or 'detached'. He was dynamic as well as emollient. His one-step-at-a-time tactics, or 'spider tactics' as Mr Nkomo saw them, were intended, as each major step was painfully taken, to encourage the expectation of success. As chairman of the conference, Carrington had been its driving force, taking the initiative at all stages.

From the outset, the whole enterprise had been a bold and risky initiative – part of its appeal to Mrs Thatcher – but, risky though it was, it had promised a greater chance of success than anything tried before. Right at the end Carrington had taken perhaps the biggest gamble of all. Britain informed the world that sanctions would be lifted, and the country returned to lawful government, under a British Governor whose task was to hold elections in which *all* parties could take part. In the middle of a shooting war, Christopher Soames had gone out to govern Rhodesia, ten days before the final agreement was reached on 21 December, and three weeks before a cease-fire which was supposed to come into effect on 28 December. During that time the wrangle over the number and location of the assembly areas, or holding camps, for the returning forces of the Patriotic Front, continued at Lancaster House.

Lord Carrington's purpose, in his carefully timed decision over Soames, was to show that Britain was still determined to take action, not fright. The immediate risk was very great, because it was still doubtful whether the final obstacle at Lancaster House, a cease-fire agreement, would be signed. The Governor had to rely on the old Rhodesian administration, its police and armed forces. Without a cease-fire, Soames would have had no instruments with which to govern and there would have been no basis for his authority. He would then have had to be withdrawn in, no doubt, humiliating circumstances.

But, for the moment at least, Rhodesia had been returned to legal government. There would be elections based upon genuine majority rule. A new constitution had been agreed upon. Therefore, the principal cause of the war had been removed. That is why, as **Lord Carrington** himself makes clear, the Foreign Secretary believed that sending out Lord Soames *before* the final agreement was signed was crucial to the whole process of bringing the London conference to a successful conclusion. In effect, it forced the Patriotic Front to an agreement.

> There was a very considerable risk in Christopher Soames going out. He took that risk, and he deserves the greatest possible credit for his courage and for his decision to go. I think it was the right decision to take because I do not believe you would really have got a conclusion to the conference *unless* he had gone out. But, there was certainly a risk. There was a risk it would blow the whole thing up. It did not. I believe it actually made it possible for a settlement.

This judgement was vindicated when, after 28 December 1979, more than a fortnight after Lord Soames's arrival in Salisbury, a cease-fire was proclaimed. It did not come into effect immediately. Fighting continued well beyond that date, but the level of conflict dropped significantly in January, and the cease-fire proved to be resilient. Rhodesia was to be spared the final spasms of war.

Once installed in Government House, in Salisbury, Lord Soames's job was to ensure that an election was held, and a campaign for it made possible. That proved extraordinarily difficult. Among the Governor's staff sent out from Britain was Robert Jackson, a Prize Fellow of All Souls, Oxford, who had been a member of Soames's Cabinet at the European Commission in Brussels. Today he is a minister of intellectual force dealing with higher education in Mrs Thatcher's government. In 1979 **Robert Jackson** went to Salisbury as Christopher Soames's Special Assistant.

> The whole exercise was done with mirrors. At its maximum the Governor's staff from Britain was very small – several hundred people. We depended on the Rhodesian administration although, of course, the guerrilla forces had come under the Queen's allegiance for the purposes of the cease-fire.

To what extent had Soames been 'educated' by the whole process at Lancaster House? The impression made there by Mugabe, for example? What possibilities had that indicated to him?

My impression was that he was not particularly involved. He was a member of the Cabinet, of course, and therefore kept in close touch. He was also a personal friend of Peter Carrington's and he had had some discussions with him. He was not involved particularly in the process itself. When he went out he had a pretty open mind about the situation. His job was to ensure that the electoral process took place.

The most important difficulty he faced arose from the fact that he had to run his administration through the existing apparatus of the Rhodesian state. For fifteen years that had been operating unconstitutionally, and outside the world community. This, of course, caused all sorts of problems. One thinks, for example, of the controversies that surrounded the 'auxiliary' forces.

The auxiliaries were Africans recruited to the Rhodesian security forces and used – and sometimes, it was alleged, abused – by them during the period of the electoral process. It was a constant battle. On the one hand, there was the world's press saying 'You are responsible for these people, what are you doing about their depredations?' and on the other hand, there was the fact that the Governor really had no effective leverage over the Rhodesian army commanders who were at the senior end of the line of command over the auxiliaries. There were many such episodes in relation to the police, in relation to the auxiliaries, and in relation to a whole series of things that the Governor was, ostensibly, responsible for, but not actually, or practically, responsible for.

Great as the difficulties undoubtedly were, there was a perception following Soames's arrival that, in spite of the intense suspicions, antagonisms and hostilities which existed, there was an underlying inevitability about a process that was now going to lead to a political solution at the polls.

On the side of the white population of Rhodesia this underlying feeling had been embodied in the position taken up by General Peter Walls, the commander of the Rhodesian forces, both at Lancaster House and subsequently, that the war was not capable of being won on the battlefield: therefore, a political settlement was necessary. Similarly, there had come the final recognition by the African leaders, Mugabe and Nkomo, that they had to engage in the political process.

Under Soames, therefore, Rhodesia found itself slipping into that more familiar, more normal, traffic of the stage – the British drama of 'de-colonization'. With all its historical overtones, this became a factor of both practical and psychological importance in Salisbury at a time when intrigue, suspicion, gossip and fear about the outcome were all intense.

> There was a great deal of suspicion of course. Salisbury was a very strange city. It had been remarkably provincial, and outside the world community, for so long. Suddenly, it was the cynosure of international politics. There were hundreds of journalists. All the hotels were full of a very cosmopolitan, polyglot crowd of people. The atmosphere was rather heady. I was very struck by the passivity of the whites, which partly reflected the exhaustion of the war. I believe that one of the most important things to remember is that the whites were almost at the end of their tether, in trying to maintain the structure created by UDI. So while there was a lot of politicking, and a great deal of gossip and intrigue, when this sudden rush of expatriates descended upon the place, underneath there was an acceptance of what they saw as, in the end, a necessary process.
>
> Some of the people who were involved in this process – not just the Governor – were playing roles which had been well scripted by history. Including, I think, the Rhodesian whites. I believe that for people who were of British formation, British history and British civilization, as the leadership of white Rhodesia was, there was always something rather peculiar and anomalous about the regime that pertained for those fifteen years which followed Smith's Unilateral Declaration of Independence – with 'President' Clifford Dupont,[1] and the peculiarly strong position which had been acquired by the military, in the shape of General Walls – almost a kind of Oliver Cromwell figure. With the return of the Queen's authority, with the presence of a Governor, with the Union Jack flying over Government House, all, as it were, returned to normality. This restoration of normality, the restoration of well-tried and familiar roles – with the Governor there, and Mary Soames[2] playing, as she did so graciously, almost a vice-regal part – created the atmosphere of a well-scripted drama. It was a drama returning to its proper course, in the final act, after being hijacked for a couple of intervening acts.

Among a raft of advisers and other personnel who arrived with Chris-

1 Rhodesia was declared a republic in March 1970. Sir Humphrey Gibbs, who, as Governor, had opposed UDI in 1965, gave up residence in Government House to Clifford Dupont, proclaimed first President of the Republic of Rhodesia.

2 Mary Soames was Winston Churchill's daughter.

topher Soames in Salisbury were those described irreverently as 'the Old and Bold'. These were the British 'observers'. There were some twenty-five of them in all. Among them were men who themselves had presided over previous transitions to independence. 'The Old and Bold' were of much experience and strong opinion. They gave advice to Christopher Soames of a particular quality and emphasis which Robert Jackson believes was a force acting upon the Governor in deciding how Britain would play the game.

> They included people like a former Professor of Race Relations at Oxford University and a number of former colonial governors. They did not play an active part in the process because they were there as observers, but certainly I found, and I think the Governor found – I know, because I was present at one or two conversations in particular – the sort of wisdom distilled by somebody like Sir Maurice Dorman, who was the chairman of the British observers of Zimbabwe's independence elections, was something which affected him.[3]
>
> *What was the wisdom Dorman distilled?*
>
> I think, fundamentally, it was by bringing home to us all, that there was a British tradition at stake here. The British tradition was a tradition of constitutionalism. Our role in Rhodesia was to see a constitutional process through to its completion, and there was the decency, as it were, and honour, that are associated with that particular British tradition. All that was an important part of the 'atmosphere'. The only places where Britain had gone, leaving a vacuum, were Palestine and Aden. It certainly seemed that there was a possibility that Rhodesia might be one of those. All of us took a certain pride in the fact that it seemed Britain was going to have a chance to see this thing through to a proper end and there was not going to be an unresolved mess in Rhodesia.
>
> *But when one comes to the outcome, what did you find was hoped for from Soames – no doubt always more than the British could deliver – but what were the expectations?*

3 Dorman's c.v. rather makes the point: Administrative Officer, Tanganyika, 1935–45; Assistant Governor, Malta, 1945; Principal Assistant Secretary, Palestine, 1947; Director of Commercial Development, Gold Coast, 1950; Colonial Secretary, Trinidad and Tobago, 1952–6; Governor of Trinidad, 1954–5; Governor and Commander-in-Chief, Sierra Leone, 1956–61; after independence, Governor General of Sierra Leone, 1961–2; Governor and Commander-in-Chief, Malta, 1962–4; after independence, Governor-General of Malta, 1964–71; Deputy Chairman of the Pearce Commission on Rhodesia, 1971–2.

There were so *many* expectations. There were some outside critics, in Africa, who felt that the whole operation was a kind of charade. We faced a great deal of criticism from Tanzania, particularly, and the Zambians. There were debates in the Security Council. Even the United States failed to back us in the United Nations debate. So, there was a certain amount of *international* suspicion about what our policy really was. There were, I suppose, different views about how it should develop. But there was a fundamental theme that ran right through it all. It was, that we had a job to do. That job was programmed by Lancaster House. The essence of it was to conduct an election so that the people of Zimbabwe could decide for themselves.

But did not Soames have two tasks, one broad – the one you have just defined – one perhaps rather narrower? The narrow one to secure, or finesse, the British interest? How was that defined at this late stage?

I am not sure it is fair to say that. The principle that governed Rhodesia was that the British interest lay in a stable transfer of power to a legitimate government, internationally recognized, and accepted *within* the country. That was the interest he was seeking to support. The basic philosophy of Lancaster House was 'Let the people decide', and it was, consistently, the policy Soames followed. There were, of course, many arguments about *how* the people were to decide, and in what sense could it be said they were making a free and unconstrained decision. It was his job to see that the election process was a fair one. There were many debates about the meaning of the word 'fair' in that context.

Carrington's determination to close a chapter of British history in a proper, honourable and dignified way and not leave 'an unresolved mess' in Rhodesia was rooted in the British constitutional tradition. However, when the crucial issue arose, during the campaign, of undue pressure being applied to the population, opponents of Lord Carrington's approach inclined to the judgement made, in another time, of Austen Chamberlain,[4] that 'he always played the game, and he always lost'. If so, it was a loss that brought more than some previous credits.

The principal critic of Carrington's settlement within the Conservative Party remained Julian Amery. Carrington had been wrong, Amery maintained, 'to weigh the pro-Soviet, totalitarian and terrorist Patriotic Front in the same scale as the pro-Western, pro-democratic government

4 Conservative statesman: Chancellor of the Exchequer 1903–6, a member of the War Cabinet in the First World War, Chancellor again in 1919–21; twice failed to secure the party leadership, in 1911 and again in 1922.

of Bishop Muzorewa'.[5] To do so was supporting the drive of Soviet imperialism in Africa.

The Governor, Christopher Soames, braced himself in particular for the return to Rhodesia, from Mozambique, of Robert Mugabe and his black spartans who, as Lord Carrington has told us, 'had done most of the fighting'. Mugabe's departure was kept under the closest surveillance by the diplomats in Maputo, where there were no less than fifty resident ambassadors. Reports of his homecoming, and the farewells which preceded it, were something to which it is known Soames paid attention in making his last judgement. Having made the final arrangements for him to fly to Salisbury, the British ambassador in Maputo, **Achilles Papadopoulos**, was on hand to watch Mugabe leave for what proved to be his ultimate triumph.

It was almost as if everybody *knew* what an important milestone Mugabe's return to Rhodesia was going to be, because we all turned up. It was as if we were seeing off a head of state. The Mozambicans had made their VIP lounge and all the other arrangements readily available to us and, indeed, somebody thought Machel may have come to the airport, behind the scenes, to shake Mugabe by the hand before he left. Anyhow, there we all were, lined up in our order of precedence, but with the conspicuous absence of the Eastern bloc. None of them was there. No Russians, no Czechs, no Poles, no East Germans, no Bulgarians. The Romanian was there, but then Romania was a bit of a maverick in this matter.

Did you deduce from that interesting moment that Soviet intelligence was not taking the confident view of the outcome that Machel and Mugabe were? Or indeed, as it seems to me you *were in reporting it to London, the feeling that Mugabe was going to win?*

I think the Russians obviously got it wrong. Why they got it wrong is not really for me to say. But they were clearly amazed, not to say shocked, when the result of the election was announced.

As you saw him off, what did you assume Mugabe's attitude would be to complying fully with Lancaster House? Particularly with the provisions about intimidation during the campaign?

I think Mugabe would have denied strenuously that he had done anything, or would do anything, in violation of the Lancaster House agreement. But, it has to be said that, after the agreement was reached,

5 From Amery's speech to the Conservative Party conference at Blackpool on 11 October 1979, during the Lancaster House conference.

and before they left London – Nkomo for Lusaka, Mugabe for Maputo – it was agreed that the forces of the Patriotic Front, in the field, would be addressed over the radio, over the BBC, by their respective leaders. They were to be told what the agreement was, and what they had to do about assembly points. Nkomo did that before he left London, but not Mugabe. I had to press Mugabe for action, but he said that he was doing it his way. His way was to send detailed instructions to his commanders in the field by runner rather than by broadcast. When the broadcast did come finally, it was all right – but he took his time.

His position could only be improved by the lapse of time – time was Mugabe's ally?

Indeed. Incidentally, I was getting complaints which all the front-line statesmen had been making to us, and which Machel made to me, more than once, about the way the Governor, Lord Soames, was using Muzorewa's auxiliaries in areas where there had been undue interference by Mugabe's men as they were marching towards the assembly points. The complaint was that Mugabe's men were 'politicizing the countryside' on the way to the assembly points. The implication was 'intimidation'. My answer to Machel, in unequivocal terms, was that if Mugabe's men did exactly as agreed at Lancaster House there would be no need for the Governor to deploy Muzorewa's auxiliaries.

As Robert Mugabe came marching home, under the Marxist banner he cherished, he was the man to watch. The Russians had backed Joshua Nkomo. In doing so perhaps they had relied overmuch on British imperial history. In the beginning, when he bought all the surface of Rhodesia, Cecil Rhodes himself had treated with the warrior caste, the Matabele, Nkomo's tribe, rather than the majority people, Mugabe's Mashona. Strangely, or perhaps *not* so strangely, this time it was the *British* who made the judgement in terms of the 'will of history' which Lenin himself might have recommended.

Like so many other chapters in Britain's post-war history, the Rhodesian settlement takes its place in what the Foreign Office diplomats might call 'The Hindsight Saga'. The fact is that almost no one confidently foresaw the overwhelming nature of Robert Mugabe's victory. That included the brooding and informed presence to the south, South Africa, as its Foreign Minister, **Pik Botha**, readily concedes.

It is all very easy with the knowledge of hindsight. Your own ambassador, and for that matter Peter Carrington – unless he intentionally misled me, which I do not believe, because I got to know him as a very straightforward and sincere man – did not predict it. Let me put it this way. I think we were *all* out. We were all out.

If one accepts that you were not alarmed by the prospect of black majority rule in Rhodesia, and that you had never supported or encouraged Smith's UDI, one presumes you were *alarmed by February and March 1980 about the possible form that black majority rule was going to take. It is an avowedly Marxist leader who is about to win the day. A man who thought that Marx explained the colonial period to him, somebody who thought Lenin's theories about imperialism were correct, and that Lenin's revolutionary focus on colonial territories was correct. What decided South Africa not to intervene when it seemed that that prospect might become a reality?*

Some two to three weeks before the election, representatives of Mr Mugabe and Mr Nkomo were in touch with representatives of South Africa abroad. I do not think it is necessary to say where. They actually sent a message to us to the effect that they were confident of winning and that, once they assumed power, they trusted that we could live together as neighbours and not allow our internal differences to dominate the necessity of co-operation between us. Now, that was an interesting message. Also at that time we were sure that Mr Mugabe was going to win, so the election result itself did not come as a surprise to us – in the end. Up to about two or three weeks before the election we still thought that Muzorewa had at least a chance of either winning, narrowly, or at least gaining quite a number of votes. I want to put this record very straight. When the result came, and Mr Mugabe won, we congratulated him. We said to ourselves, 'Look, we've gone through this before. Let's give it a chance.' There was a request, I think, for a ninety million rand loan, trade was being carried on as before, and in general there was not the exodus of whites into South Africa as many expected. We would have *preferred* differently. I would be misleading you, if I said otherwise. Of *course* we would have preferred Muzorewa as Prime Minister. But Mugabe won. That was that. We were not very happy with the *way* he had won, and the intimidation that was rife, sure, but that was then beside the point. That was history.

Already history, at that point? What attitude did you take to Soames, who after all did have the powers, as Governor, of disqualification of parties practising intimidation?

We knew he would not. It was just not 'on'. It was not realistic, it was not practical.

Why was it not on?

It was the way it went. The momentum, throughout, was to recognize the election. I think many people in Britain, and in your parliament, did not like it at all. But that would have started a war all over again. But, I do not think the result would have been much different, even if the supervision of the elections could have been tightened up.

Many think that Rhodesia hovered on the brink of a coup, for a few weeks in February and March 1980. Supposing the result had been closer, or more confused, might South Africa have given its support to annulling the outcome of the election?

No, no. Look, I know it might be interesting to a person like you and I appreciate your interest in the matter, but I'm not given to that kind of speculation. It was gone, it was over, a new era had started and that was that.

It certainly had. That's why I am asking. Would I be right to suppose that it was the margin of Mugabe's victory which made such action out of the question?

I was never part of any discussion within South African government ranks about doing anything to change the result.

There was, of course, no place for the Foreign Minister in such affairs. What talk there was of a coup in Harare, to reverse the election result, lost the name of action.

On the side of the whites in Rhodesia, realization that they could not win the war and that a political solution had to be found was implicit both in General Wall's presence, and in the role he had played during the London conference. Lord Carrington pays tribute to Walls, 'almost a Cromwellian figure' in Robert Jackson's estimation, as a steadying influence throughout. The military had acquired a particularly strong position in Ian Smith's Rhodesia and their support had been indispensable to Lord Carrington. That support was largely conditioned by hopes and expectations that Bishop Muzorewa would do well enough, and that Mr Nkomo might come in to broaden the internal settlement and so, effectively, exclude Robert Mugabe from power.

At Lancaster House the parties to the Smith–Muzorewa 'internal' settlement had fought for powers to be given to Lord Carrington to disqualify those who practised intimidation. The fact that Carrington had those powers, and the possibility that he might use them, helped keep white Rhodesians, and the Rhodesian armed forces in particular, reasonably content about the electoral process. When the British decided not to deploy those powers, there was a moment when everyone held their breath: among them, **Lord Carrington**, who recalls his own apprehensions when the election result was announced.

I did not really know *what* was going to happen. I thought that there would be deep disappointment in Conservative circles at the fact that Mr Mugabe had won the election, and I was by no means sure that there would not be a backlash in Rhodesia, from the whites, which might lead to a coup. I was wrong about the reaction in England to it because, in spite of the intimidation, there was really massive evidence that the people of Rhodesia did want Mugabe. I think I *was* right about my fear of the backlash in Rhodesia. I suspect that, but for General Walls, there might very well have been a coup, and I think that people owe a great deal to General Walls. He had a very rough and difficult time. He behaved as honourably as anybody I know.

He feels, apparently, that you betrayed him.

I am afraid he does, yes. But I do not think I did.

But how do you answer him?

I do not see why I betrayed him. It does not seem to me that I betrayed him.

He appears to think that we had another plan in being, that our real intention was to bring in Nkomo to broaden the base of Smith's internal settlement, Smith being out of the way.

That was one of the possibilities in an election which did not produce a *majority*. But if the election produced the majority, such as it did for Mugabe, there was no way in which that could happen. There was no way in which Mr Nkomo would have joined.

The crucial thing then was the unequivocal nature, at least in numerical terms, of Mugabe's majority? The sheer size of it?

Yes. It was overwhelming. There was no way in which you could expect Mr Nkomo, or anybody else, to form a coalition in opposition. I suspect that Mr Nkomo would have been quite happy to do it, but there was no way in the face of that election result in which it could happen.

A definitude of words at Lancaster House has been unable to define what was to be considered a 'free and fair' election, in the heart of Africa, in the immediate aftermath of a bitter civil war. One senior Foreign Office official, Sir John Graham, when challenged about this at Lancaster House, had an Africanized simile ready to hand. 'Free and fair' was like an elephant – it resisted close definition. However, all would recognize one when they saw it.

As the fighting wound down and the death toll dropped in January 1980, from fifty to five a day, the election process itself became 'the continuation of politics by other means'. In his mastery of these other means, Mr Mugabe won hands-down in orchestrating the intense struggle for power which the electoral process entailed. In **Robert Mugabe**'s own view, therefore, what determined the final outcome and his personal triumph?

I think it was the work we had done. Our opponents – Nkomo is one such critic – believe it was a fact that there was intimidation on our side. None of that at all could have swung the pendulum in our favour. That alone could never have done it. It was the work we did during the war. We combined military action with political work, politicizing the people, getting them to accept ZANU, and ZAPU, in their areas. It was ZANU, ZANU, ZANU in all areas in which we operated. Do not forget that Nkomo's ZAPU came into this war much later than we did. They had suffered a setback whereby Chikerema and Nyandoro[6] split away from them and it took them time to reorganize themselves. It was not until 1978 really that they came into the war with some effect. Before that it was a ZANU, ZANU, ZANU affair.

Nkomo was, and he still is, incredulous that you could win seats in Matabeleland, in Nkomo's own strongholds, and yet that he, an internationally recognized leader of African nationalism over many years, could win none in the part of Rhodesia which you *come from, in Mashonaland.*

He did win one. In the area of Mashonaland West, my home province for that matter.

'It was not just intimidation,' he said, 'we lost a candidate, and eighteen to twenty party workers killed by ZANU outside the assembly points. They were given the task to see to it that everyone in that area voted ZANU.'

Ah, well, that is what he says. But really there was lots of intimidation from *Muzorewa* forces. He should talk about those more. They had been trained to kill, and they went all out. All kinds of things happened and all kinds of devices, and efforts to prevent our smooth operation were used by the Rhodesian forces at that time. Bombs everywhere

6 James Chikerema was acting chairman of Nkomo's ZAPU; George Nyandoro was another 'moderate' nationalist who eventually was a member of Muzorewa's official delegation at Lancaster House.

in our way – bombing buses, and doing it in a manner they felt would be interpreted as the action of ZANLA.[7]

I don't forget when I ask about intimidation that there were assassination attempts, planned or aborted, on your own life.[8] *But, would you agree as a Marxist applying Marxist techniques, in which the popular will is politicized – then that was the reality. Eddison Zvobgo, one if your ministers, mentioned subsequently*[9] *that British intelligence had said repeatedly that there were six to eight thousand ZANLA forces – your forces – inside Rhodesia. 'We chose', he said, 'to declare twenty thousand because, if everybody thought we had eight, and we declared and were willing to offer* twenty, *then we could have no others left.' Zvobgo made the real point arising: 'In fact' he said, 'we had a very large army left. They remained political commissars in the country* simply to ensure that we would win the election.'

Yes. Sure. They became commissars, political workers, organizing. They had no arms – most of them – during the election, and we sent them round. They became political commissars. We used lots of our ZANLA personnel, not as armed people, but as political commissars, because every ZANLA combatant, you see, was made politically conscious and 'ideologized' in a very big way. You could just pick anyone, during the struggle, and they could give you what our political, and ideological, position was.

That, surely, is the point. What you would claim to be a superior technique does not separate political and military activity?

No. No. It doesn't, of course.

The Foreign Office had not disguised from ministers the view of its officials, held from the beginning of the intensive Rhodesian diplomacy in 1979, that 'the Radicals were likely to win'. But, at least until Mugabe's return to Rhodesia, after Lancaster House, when the obvious enthusiasm of his reception impressed official minds, the general expectation had remained that no one would win an outright victory. There was the belief, to recall Sir Ian Gilmour's words, that 'Joshua might move around a bit' – in other words, that Mr Nkomo, 'or parts of Nkomo', would come in to deepen and widen the internal settlement. This more or less ordained that the suspicions and antagonisms of the long struggle were

7 ZANLA was the fighting force of Mr Mugabe's party, ZANU.

8 Ken Flower, then head of CIO, the Rhodesian intelligence service, mentions two such attempts, both aborted, in Fort Victoria in February 1980 (Ken Flower, *Serving Secretly* (London, John Murray, 1987), p. 257).

9 In the Granada television series *End of Empire.*

carried forward to be invested, finally, in the issue of disqualification. To ban, or not to ban, parties which coerced the voters? It was a matter for lasting reproach by all those who felt persuaded, or who had persuaded themselves, that the British objective was, broadly speaking, 'Anybody but Mugabe', that **Lord Carrington** did not invoke the powers he had sought for the Governor, and been granted, at Lancaster House.

> Christopher Soames was the Governor, and he was the man on the spot. It was a difficult decision. It was *my* decision, of course, or rather the government's decision, but it was *his* advice, and it was difficult advice to give. What he said, and I am sure that he was right, was that there *was* intimidation, and very unpleasant intimidation. But it was not, by any means, confined to Mr Mugabe's supporters. There was intimidation *all round*, though I think probably he would have said there was more intimidation from the Mugabe faction than from the others. But, since there was intimidation all round it was really better not to disqualify one party when the others were guilty, even though possibly not so guilty.
>
> *Were we just unwilling to face the possibilities of disqualification – it would have been chaotic?*
>
> Well, I do not know what would have happened if there had been disqualification. Certainly, the cease-fire would have broken down, and you would have had the greatest possible difficulty. It was obviously an option, but it was not an option, I think, which anybody would have wished to take unless the circumstances were so bad that they felt they ought to. Then you would have had to weigh the consequences of doing it.

With people from all over the world on the spot and watching the election campaign, Lord Carrington's determination that the British should be irreproachable rubbed uncomfortably against the pledge that all should have a fair chance to put their electoral support to the test.

Polling began on 27 February 1980 and closed five days later. The sizeable British contingent – servicemen, diplomats, civil servants and 'the Old and Bold' – on hand to see the election process through included five hundred British policemen specially flown out. The bobbies lent a metropolitan touch to the polling stations.

Because it was widely believed that Soames intended to use the powers he had to deal with intimidation, to disqualify candidates, to suspend the election in certain areas, there was heavy pressure applied to him to use these powers against Mr Mugabe's party. There were heated exchanges between British officials and senior staff of the Rhodesian armed forces, General Walls in particular, over the disqualification issue at this time. Among those who petitioned Soames directly concerning Robert Mugabe's campaigning methods was **Air Vice-Marshal Harold Hawkins**, who had played a significant part in pursuit of an agreement at Lancaster House as Muzorewa's foreign affairs adviser and the representative of his government in Pretoria.

> I went to Soames myself and told him that people whose views I trusted, like Ken Flower[10] and others, had given me specific instances of this intimidation. I said to him, 'This is against the whole spirit of the agreement, and action should be taken.' He said to me, and these were his exact words, 'I hear what you say, but they are *all* doing it!' And I said, 'Yes. But not on the same scale.' That is the way it was left. Nothing happened. Bishop Muzorewa stormed out, of course, saying he was dealing with crooks. Some of the chiefs of staffs' exchanges were quite heated because I think they expected to find rather stronger action as they were providing the muscle to maintain law and order while the process was taking place.
>
> *How did you understand Soames's reluctance to use his powers to disqualify?*
>
> I think he just wanted to get it over with. They obviously could not stay for ever. They wanted the election to proceed and get the whole exercise done. I think they did it as fairly as they could, according to their lights. They did not have sufficient intelligence of their own and they were not prepared to accept, unequivocally, what the commanders and the head of the intelligence organization were telling them.
>
> *Even so, what were your own reactions when it became clear Mugabe had won as hugely as he did?*
>
> Total dismay. Total dismay. Not knowing the Patriotic Front, except for seeing them at Lancaster House, or how they intended to behave thereafter, I thought such a sweeping victory was probably very bad news indeed.

The Governor, Christopher Soames, in deciding not to use his powers to ban, in those last tense weeks before the final result, had determined that it would be wise not to face a storm Britain could not weather. The Lord Privy Seal, **Sir Ian Gilmour**, was the Cabinet minister who answered for the Rhodesia policy in the House of Commons. He recalls

10 Flower was retained in his position as head of Rhodesian intelligence by Mugabe after the election.

how this, the last big decision of the Rhodesia diplomacy, to ban or not to ban, was considered and taken.

> Primarily, it was left to the man on the spot, Christopher Soames. My own view was that if you disqualified Mugabe you made the election a farce. No doubt there was some intimidation, no doubt also intimidation did not only come from Mugabe, or from Nkomo. It was on *all* sides. To my mind, if you had disqualified him you would not only have made the election a farce, you would have stultified the entire Lancaster House agreement. Nevertheless, there were powerful, influential and respectable voices in favour of disqualifying him. I think the primary credit for disregarding those must go, almost entirely, to Christopher Soames. He disregarded them and allowed the election to go ahead. I have no doubt that decision was right.
>
> *We know that Christopher Soames had a couple of hours, most of them alone, with Mugabe at the end of February, just before the final verdict of the election was to become known, in March, and they were clearly a very important two hours. Soames had to refer that to Carrington in London. What do you recall of that decision to cut the Gordian knot taken, in the end, by Lord Carrington for the government?*
>
> It was quite a difficult decision, but I am sure it was the right one. To have disqualified would have nullified all that we were trying to do. Although there was undoubtedly intimidation, there was intimidation in every single election in England in the eighteenth century – and a good deal in the nineteenth century. No one thought of nullifying those! A lot of the pressure for nullifying the election and disqualifying Mugabe was just because people did not want him to win. It went far wider than just the fact that his followers were intimidating people. As far as I know, there has not been an election in Africa, or indeed practically anywhere else, without intimidation. So, it was no doubt a brave decision by Peter Carrington, but I'm absolutely convinced it was the right one.

The discovery that black Rhodesians were not an immature race incapable of political action was represented in the political and military ascendancy of Mugabe, and the recognition of that by Carrington and Soames. So it was that, in the last tense days of February 1980 leading up to the election, Soames asked **Robert Mugabe** to come to Government House in Salisbury. And there, they talked, alone.

'Beware of documents,' said Clemenceau, 'they are pitfalls for historians'; but, in any case, it will be a long time before the official record of the Rhodesian diplomacy becomes public. Here, instead, is the future President of Zimbabwe's personal recollection of the intriguing and successful encounter between himself and Soames, and the formation of what, thereafter, became an enduring personal relationship.

The meeting you are referring to was the one when he finally said he had decided not to ban us, and that we could participate in the election. The one man he had banned from campaigning was Enos Nkala,[11] but he too was free to present himself as a candidate for the election. Well, it was a great relief. I said to him 'Fine. We are very grateful for that, and I think it is a great gesture. It shows magnanimity on the part of the British government.' I think that was the one moment when I grew closer to him and he perhaps to me. I appreciated, in spite of all that had happened, the quarrel, the near-fight, that there was still some greatness in his soul. He had ignored, if not defied, the advice which some of his advisers, his henchmen, had given him. We were aware of that because we had, in fact, one or two telling us the story from the inside. There was a friend of ours, who was in the British team, telling us not even to raise our hopes publicly too high but to say, rather, that we hoped to win, not a *majority* of seats, but perhaps forty or so, because if our own expressed hope that we would win a majority of the seats were *believed*, 'then the desire and tendency to ban you would strengthen'. Christopher Soames was actually saying that he had people who were bitterly opposed to ZANU advising him. He defied that, and this made him quite a great man to us.

When Soames called you in, and you had that one and a half hours alone with him on disqualification, and he said 'I am not going to disqualify you', do you think that he had concluded, by then, that you were going to win as you did?

I do not think so. I think that their intelligence, which was very faulty and misleading, had led them to believe that we would get less than half the seats and that, if we did, then the rest of the parties, with the rest of votes, could be put together against us. He admitted this to me the last time he came to see us. We invited them to dinner, he and Mary Soames. He said to me, 'Do you know what we were going to do if you had *not* won more than 50 per cent of the votes?' I said, 'No.' And Mary was saying, 'Oh Christopher! Do we *have* to go back over those things?' She was trying to prevent him and he was angry,

11 Enos Nkala was the Treasurer of ZANU(PF). He was banned from campaigning on 18 February. His addresses maintained that if ZANU were defeated at the polls, the war would continue.

saying 'You always do this to me, I won't have it.' So he went on and said, 'We were going to ask Nkomo and Muzorewa, and the others, to come together to form a government and exclude you.' That was his thinking at that time. And I'm sure, I know, that he regretted he ever had it.

Can you elaborate on the bond between you? On the face of it a rather unlikely one.

It strengthened after the election when he called me and asked me to form a government. Then, with this victory in our hands, we had to look into the future. I said to him, 'I want you to be with me. I don't want you to leave us now. I have great experience in leading a party as a liberation movement but I have never run a government before. You have lots of experience in that direction. You have been in various governments and I want to have the benefit of your experience, so that you can assist me. Stay here and help me.' Christopher said to me, 'Really?' I said, 'Yes. I mean it. The past is all gone. We have fought and it is all past. Now we must work together and mould the country together.' He said he was going to send all this to Lord Carrington, and in no time the message came to say that Lord Carrington agreed and he could remain for a few more weeks.

It is said that until the very last moment, even after that first discussion with him when he told you that you were not to be banned, until he actually asked you to form the government you were frankly disbelieving that you would.

I knew that he would ask me, even if reluctantly, but was forced to do so by the size of our victory. When I was asked at a press conference outside my house what I would do if I did not get an absolute majority and Lord Soames put together a government from which I was left out, I said that we were going to ensure that he had only one choice. That would be to call upon ZANU to form a government. That is what we did by our campaign and our victory at the polls.

But we also feared, in spite of that victory, that there was a possibility of the British acquiescing in a military takeover. To tell you the truth, every day we felt something might happen. We felt something might happen to prevent us going to election and to prevent people from voting. We then felt something might happen to prevent the vote being announced. Even after I had been called to form a government, and *had* formed it, we still feared that the South Africans, working with the former Rhodesians, General Walls and others, might just do something. I may say that is one reason why we felt we needed the British presence. It was to ward off this kind of action.

The exchanges between Mr Mugabe and Lord Soames proved a watershed in the history of Britain's last colony in Africa. The meeting at which Mr Mugabe was told by the Governor that he was not to be proscribed cast a benign light over subsequent events and the relationship between Zimbabwe and Britain. Robert Mugabe proved a tactful winner. He created a climate of reconciliation in which a sizeable proportion of whites decided to stay on.

It was Walter Bagehot who said that the British nation was fair, but that 'a free nation is rarely quick of apprehension. It only comprehends what is familiar to it, what comes into its own experience, what squares with its own thoughts.' To the British, *vox populi* had become *vox dei*, expressed as 'one man, one vote'. But Africa, in the long history of mass de-colonization, almost always made that 'one vote, one man'. Mr Mugabe waited only the agreed period before making Zimbabwe a one-party state, announced as conforming to Lenin's principles of 'democratic centralism'. Lord Carrington's settlement was able to preserve only the memory of British constitutionalism, the green leather benches, the Speaker's mace, the paraphernalia of Parliament. The owl of Minerva spreads its wings only with the falling dusk. Looking back, in great wisdom, what did **Lord Carrington** believe were the chances of a settlement, when he launched the Rhodesian diplomacy?

If you had really asked me what I thought was going to happen, I would have said to you that it would fail and that I would have my head chopped off as a result. Not by the Prime Minister but, you know, by the public thinking this was a pretty rotten failure and we ought never to have tried it and we'd better get rid of the guy.

That it was a sell-out?

Not a sell-out, so much as a failure. The right wing of the Conservative Party certainly would have laid a considerable stress upon the fact that it was a sell-out, or an attempted sell-out – which, of course, they did anyway.

Which they did anyway, and some of these people were Mrs Thatcher's closest political friends.

Some of them were my closest friends as far as that goes. Even if they are not necessarily *politically* my closest friends.

The fact is that Mr Mugabe has moved towards a one-party state, avowedly on Marxist–Leninist principles. Does that give you pause, in hindsight, as you look back on it?

I think he would always have *said* that. But I do not think there is any indication that the white businessman feels that the economy, generally, is going to be a Marxist one, as of now. He may want to move that way, but I would not think he would move that way if he thought that it was going to ruin the country.

But the point is that you did not then, and you do not now, think that you were importing the grandchildren of Lenin to the railway station in Salisbury.

No. Not then, and nor do I now.

With the coming of independence, Cecil Rhodes's triumphal statue was removed with alacrity from the heart of Salisbury, now Harare. President Nyerere of Tanzania is known to have said to Robert Mugabe that he had 'inherited a jewel'. Rhodesia incorporated the last great colonizing impulses of the British. It was an archetype of historical energy. As a result of Rhodes's ideals and ruthlessness there are British towns and cities in the African bush. And, if there was greed, there was much good in the adventure. What is **President Robert Mugabe**'s, and the African ambition? Is it to replicate and sustain those energies? Or does it aspire to be different?

It is to continue the process of development with guidance from the new political thinking. The country must continue to be run on the basis of democracy. The benefits that accrue from the development must be equitably shared. This is why we believe that socialism yields that modality of sharing which is more equitable, perhaps, than the modality of the capitalist system. We feel that the British or, if you prefer, the sons and daughters of the British who came here, and who are still here, are free to remain as part of our society. We have a lot still to learn from them because of the experience they have. But we would want them to impart that experience as part of our society and as *Zimbabweans.* We want them, as Zimbabweans, to continue to work hard together with everybody else in a *new* socio-economic order. Hence we feel that the level of development we have inherited from the past is no longer adequate. The population continues to increase. The demands of our society continue to grow.

Your revolutionary movement, as you acknowledge, never had time to reach the cities and towns in order to politicize the urban worker. It was largely conducted in the rural areas where the mass of the population lives. What difficulties do you see for yourself there in raising expectations in rural areas which cannot be fulfilled?

Fortunately for us it is true that the struggle, for a start, was in urban areas. That was when it was still a political struggle and we ran political parties – nationalist movements that agitated and used arguments from the platform in the hope that we could appeal successfully to the British government for a constitutional conference. But, once the struggle went beyond that stage and became military, then it was in the rural areas because we had to use those as our launching pads, to expand the fight into other areas. So, there was greater politicization of the people in rural areas and less in the urban ones. As a result you get an imbalance in the political understanding of the two communities. The urban dweller, the worker, here is much more exacting in his demands on government than the rural one. The rural person is much more patient and more understanding. Even though the level of education is in favour of the urban people.

There must be accelerated development in all fields. There must be *fairness.* Land must be shared. That is why we have a resettlement programme. We cannot deprive those who have large farms, arbitrarily, of those farms. We are going to acquire land. We must abide by legality, but also by the requirement of fair play. In agriculture, in mining, in industry, there has to be a concerted effort right across the board to raise the level of our development. We feel that the infrastructure we have at the moment is really better than that which other African countries have inherited. It makes it easier for us to transform our economy. Using this legacy of the energies you mentioned, which are visible, we should I think be much more ahead of the rest of Africa and sooner or later become a developed country. We still have lots to learn even from Britain. I say even from Britain because it is our past colonial master. We have developed new relations with other countries but we find problems in developing good relations with the United States. It has got quite a strange attitude, different from that of Britain. They don't want to be criticized in any way. They take offence easily. Even though our ideology is socialist we still feel there are areas where we can be associated with capitalist countries. Anyway, today you have the Soviet Union seeking a great association with the United States, so who are we to refuse a similar association in our own context?

The settlement produced by Lord Carrington and Mrs Thatcher at Lancaster House was acknowledged internationally as a remarkable triumph. It left no devastated regions of the mind in Britain where it was, for so many years, the most emotional issue in British politics. It is hardly surprising that there is still no agreement on the key points between Lord Carrington and his arch-opponents at home over the outcome.

For Julian Amery, the British colonial achievement was indivisible from his concept of Britain itself as a nation. More than that: it was not just a matter for affection but for a perpetual lamp. In addition to which, **Julian Amery** considered the dowry Mr Mugabe has brought to Zimbabwe may be too small for lasting harmony.

I think the failure of the settlement, the economic problems that are mounting, the formation of a one-party state, increasingly Marxist in its orientation, the troubles in Matabeleland – all these things have rather proved that the line of policy which the successive governments took was wrong. This is increasingly recognized. If you look back – you brought in 'Munich' once or twice in our talk – the general reaction to Munich was one of enthusiastic acceptance, by the country. Three years later it was a dirty word. All through the Second World War, and in the Cold War that followed the war, there was a great revulsion against appeasement of the Munich character. Even 'Yalta' became a dirty word. This went on, really, until the Suez operation. I believe it was the failure of that operation that knocked the stuffing out of the political classes. Had we won that battle, I think the whole British and European policy would have been changed. I remember the French Prime Minister of the time,[12] just before the operation, saying if we, Britain and France, win we will not just save our interests in the Middle East and North Africa, we shall build a united Europe, and we shall have shown that we can stand up to the Americans and the Russians. It was not done. From Suez onwards the rot set in, in the thinking, or rather the *feeling* of the British political classes. And then, the failure of the Rhodesian settlement, in my judgement, is now widely accepted and there has been a revulsion against appeasement, which was made very clear at the time of the Falklands. One has to, has to face it. Had we not had a strong and decisive leader in Margaret Thatcher, I think the political classes would have jumped at the opportunities that were presented of appeasing the Argentine dictator.

That suggests that, in effect, Lord Carrington was forced out over the Falklands crisis because of what happened in Rhodesia?

Yes, in a sense he was. It is unfair to say it, because I don't hold him responsible for the invasion of the Falklands, although I think the Foreign Office should have foreseen it; but I suppose you could say that, ironically, it was Bishop Muzorewa's revenge.

There are wheels within wheels as the British come to terms with the

12 Guy Mollet.

evolution from empire and Commonwealth to membership of the European Community, and in the use of charged words like 'appeasement' and 'Munich', you can hear them. As we know today, from the Franks Report,[13] it was the strains within the governing party over Rhodesia which deferred Cabinet discussion and decision of the recommended policy to be rid of the far-away Falklands. When Argentina invaded, Britain went to war because it *had* to, but also in the aftermath of the Rhodesian outcome, and in a spirit of 'No, dammit, the Falklands are *ours*.' Lord Carrington, one of the most dynamic and effective Foreign Secretaries for many years, resigned after the Argentine invasion of the Falkland Islands. And, it might be felt, 'Long stood Sir Bedevere revolving many memories.' When the Falklands crisis blew up, and as between two views of Britain in the world, was **Lord Carrington**, in reality, forced out of the government over Rhodesia?

I would not accept that I was forced out. I mean, I don't think that is what happened. But, for a number of reasons, I was not very popular with the right wing of the Conservative Party. Probably, Rhodesia was one of the chief ones, and that certainly did not help.

What view is justified of the settlement?

I think it has turned out very much better than anybody might have supposed. Certainly, the anxieties that we all had after the election have not really been borne out. I think everybody would agree with that. Of course, one does not agree with, or applaud, everything that has happened in Zimbabwe but, by and large, I think it has turned out a good deal better than anybody would have suggested at that time.

It is said that when it was all over the Prime Minister invited those most intimately involved to Downing Street and thanked them in a speech lasting five minutes, of which one minute was spent on the 'thanks', and four minutes on Cecil Rhodes.

I do not remember that. I remember her being extremely generous about it and very complimentary. I think she was not, of course – nobody was – ever expecting Mugabe was going to win the election in the way he did. But, I think we all felt that this was the best solution we could expect to get. I think she shared that view.

In what way had we retrieved British interests?

13 The report of a Committee of Privy Councillors chaired by Lord Franks set up to review British policy concerning the Falkland Islands following the Argentine invasion of 1982 and the war that followed (HMSO, 1983).

> Well, we had settled the problem. As a result it ceased to be a running sore in our relations with other members of the Commonwealth. I think we avoided the break-up of the Commonwealth. I think that we avoided an appalling row in the European Community, and probably in the United Nations. I think we certainly avoided a break with President Carter's administration in the United States. I also think that, at that particular time, I suppose 80 per cent of the work done in the Foreign Office was connected with the Rhodesian question – and there were *other* issues which I thought the Foreign Office ought to have been dealing with. Like the European Community and the Budget problem, and the Middle East, and all the rest of it. The settlement enabled these other things to be pursued with more vigour than they had been in the past.

As it had done in the days of Queen Victoria's empire, once again, it seemed, Rhodesia had focused the guiding principles of British policy. Europe was to be Britain's acre now. A previous occupant of Lord Carrington's chair in the Foreign Office, that zealous retrencher Lord Palmerston, had argued in the previous century that 'Britain had no need of vast imperial possessions any more than a rational man with an estate in the North of England and a residence in the South would wish to possess all the inns on the Great North Road.'

Cecil Rhodes had changed all that, at Kimberley. Only ninety years before, Rhodes had stood in the front rank of those who had shaped the world in his time. In doing so, he had made his way from the Cape to the Zambesi among Africa's iron-age monarchies and nude tribes. As the British followed him into the scramble for Africa they reached there a peak of energy and fulfilment. British colonization of southern Africa became the tail that wagged the Whitehall dog. That 'immense and brooding spirit', as Kipling wrote of Rhodes, 'shall quicken and control'.[14] But, after 'Suez', retrenchment quickened rather than control. Rhodes's spirit did not long outlast him. Margaret Thatcher paid him the tribute of a lingering look behind, and the final outcome in Rhodesia, which she recognized as a necessary compromise, and had pursued as a personal objective, was a deflection of her own instinctive sympathies.

In its claim on British emotions the issue of Rhodesia was a curtain-call of empire. It was a painful step on Britain's journey back to what that more truly immense and brooding spirit, Churchill, had said – even before the end of the Second World War – must now become Britain's 'prime care': Britain's former and older constituency on the continent

14 Rudyard Kipling, 'The Burial'. C. J. Rhodes was buried in the Matopos hills on 10 April 1902.

of Europe.[15] In the matter of their return to Europe the British have managed to restrain their enthusiasms. Mrs Thatcher, preferring to be linked, rather than comprised, has baulked at the European priority established by her predecessor as Conservative leader, Edward Heath. When it comes to 'Europe', the Prime Minister remains a churchgoing agnostic.

The last retreat from Africa therefore was accompanied by the revival of new purpose, if not clarity over future directions. Three weeks after the formal transfer of power to independent Zimbabwe on 17 April 1980, the Prime Minister told the Scottish Conservative conference, 'We are once more a nation capable of action rather than reaction.' A new spirit of combat was soon to be abroad in the making and the conduct of Britain's foreign policy. The settlement of the Rhodesia question had launched Margaret Thatcher into the international arena with a stunning diplomatic achievement.

15 Churchill wrote a remarkable minute at a remarkable moment in the Second World War, on 21 October 1942 to his Foreign Secretary Anthony Eden. It was two days before Alexander and Montgomery opened the offensive which led to the Battle of El Alamein. 'I must admit that my thoughts rest primarily in Europe, in the revival of the glory of Europe, the parent continent of modern nations and of civilization. It would be a measureless disaster if Russian barbarism overlaid the culture and independence of the ancient states of Europe. Hard as it is to say now, I trust the European family may act unitedly as one, under a Council of Europe in which the barriers between nations will be greatly minimized and unrestricted travel will be possible. I hope to see the economy of Europe studied as a whole. Of course we shall have to work with the Americans in many ways and in the greatest ways, but Europe must be our prime care . . .'

Index